For Joan -
with Best Wishes -
Happy Entertaining!
Always,
Sherry Bush
August 15, 2022

All photography by L'amour,
specialists in fine photographic art
and portraiture

Kansas City, Missouri

the newlyweds guide to entertaining

by Sherry Galanti Klein

Mesa Books
Overland Park, Kansas USA

 A catalog record for this book is under application at the Library of Congress, Washington, DC.

ISBN 0-9728949-0-X

Printed in the United States of America
First Edition

the newlyweds guide to entertaining

This book was born of the author's frustration.

I wanted to buy a guide book on entertaining for a special young couple about to be married, but I couldn't find one anywhere. So I decided to write one!

This book is dedicated to newlyweds.

With gratitude to my many friends for inspiration, editing and taste-testing on demand.

With special appreciation to Eric Klein for editing; to Pamela Klein and Jay Widman for recipe ideas; to Vicki and Andrew Widman for sharing and testing recipes; and to Marshall Widman for his continued confidence and assistance, always.

table of contents

Welcome

Congratulations! You have tied the knot, gotten hitched, your dream has come true - you have gotten married! Your sweetheart has become your official spouse. You have had, on average, 2.5 bridal showers where you have received, on average, approximately 75 kitchen appliances, pots, pans, dishes and gadgets. (Not to mention the beautiful wedding presents for which you might still be writing Thank You notes.)

What will you do with all of these pots, pans, dishes and gadgets? Why, of course, you will entertain... all of those family and friends who have given you the gifts in the first place. But how? You've never done this. The many pages of this book will be your guide. It is intended to be used by both bride and groom. How much more fun as you start your lives together!

The intention of this endeavor is not to help you become "made from scratch" gourmet cooks or home interior design experts. Rather, it is to help you welcome others into your home with delicious meals and inviting table décor quickly, easily and with minimum expense. I want you to have time and energy to enjoy your guests... and each other. Simply put... I want you to have fun! And...

Congratulations!! SGK

basics and set-ups

There have been many books written on entertaining. Most involve making detailed lists of foods to have in your pantry and foods to buy, carefully determining guest lists, then painstakingly choosing where each guest should sit, etc., etc.... By the time you finally have the party you are exhausted. My method is different: do the bare minimum in preparation in order to have the maximum amount of fun. A relatively tidy house is important, but spotless is not. The bathroom should be clean (more on that later...), but probably no one is going into that spare bedroom, so just close the door. If necessary make a cute little sign that says "Please don't enter!! The stuffed animals are sleeping." Your family and friends will understand. They are just happy to be invited at all.

This is not a cookbook! There is no shortage of any type of cookbook you might imagine. Yet entertaining does involve having good food, and having good food often involves cooking to some degree... hence, the many recipes included here. But the recipes in this Guide are very different than most. They have all been carefully selected to have as few ingredients as possible, and these ingredients should be easy to find at your local grocery. Assembling and opening cans and frozen packages is usually the most difficult part. The instructions should be clear... although please glance at all parts of the recipe before starting. There really are some very helpful tips.

By experience I know that the details of a party are really not that important. The main factors for success are warm and gracious hosts and plenty of reasonably good food and drink. Did you understand that word... reasonably? Please do not expect to become a gourmet cook your first year of marriage. Won't happen... and not necessary.

Relax... enjoy... have fun with your guests... have fun with each other. That's the purpose of this book!

Now, having said that, there are a few things you DO need to do...

Yes, you must clean the bathrooms. If you don't have time or energy to do a full scrub job, just make sure the sink and toilet areas are wiped with a wet cloth, all trash is emptied, and the floor is swept or vacuumed. A new roll of toilet paper, fresh guest towels (either cloth or disposable) and a fresh bar of soap are also nice. If you have time, polish the mirror with a little glass cleaner, remove all items that are obviously personal and light a small votive candle.

You can choose to just tidy the main areas where you know your guests will be, or you can use entertaining as a good excuse to clean your entire home. It's your choice. Either way, make sure your bed is made so that you will have a place to put the coats.

Close the doors to the rooms you don't want seen.

Candles.... bring out all your candles... different sizes, different shapes, even different colors if you like. The flickering lights will bring warmth and a sense of intimacy to your gathering. Do be sure to keep an eye on all lit candles, making sure tapers remain upright and away from decorations and napkins. Votives in glass containers are nice to place around the room as you won't have to worry as much about fire hazards.

Do you have a favorite wine bottle... perhaps from your honeymoon? Carefully wash and dry the empty bottle and fill with lamp oil and a special wick available at stores where candles are sold. This is a unique decoration for the bar area, or for the dining table when a dinner with wine is served. Another colorful addition to the table or bar is a piece of your stemware filled with hard, unwrapped candy such as jelly beans surrounding a plastic or metal-encased tealight candle placed in the center.

And just what is the proper way to set the table?

There is actually no proper way to officially set the table. As long as you have the basic eating utensils laid out in a convenient way for you and your guests, you have many options. The traditional way is first to cover the table with a tablecloth or individual placemats, then set one placesetting in front of each guest's chair. Set the dinner plate in the center of each area; place folded napkin to the left with fork (or forks) on top of napkin (smaller fork to the left); and place knife, then spoon (or spoons) to the right of the plate. The knife (with blade facing plate) should be between the plate and the spoons. Water glass traditionally in front of plate on the right and wine or juice glass next to the water glass. Hope I haven't confused you yet. At any rate, I am here to tell you it does not matter!

Be creative with all of your beautiful dishes, glassware, eating utensils, napkins, etc. Again I tell you it really doesn't matter where the various plates, glasses and forks are as long as your guests will have a reasonable idea exactly what is intended for their use. The important thing is simply to have the necessary dishes, utensils, napkins, etc. available. After that, let your imagination be your guide.

Simple, but pretty: Place silverware on top of napkins and tie with pretty ribbons; lay across dinner plates. For a casual dinner, use fluffy white paper towels with your favorite napkin holders. Not sure about how to fold the napkins? Fluff the napkins inside of each wine or water glass.

If you received all of your dishes, silverware and glassware that you registered for before you were married, by all means use them. Enjoy these beautiful gifts as much as possible, for they are meant to be used. But, if you are like most bridal couples, you received only part (if any at all) of what you have chosen and will have a lifetime to add to your collection. Please don't wait until the collection is complete before you start to enjoy what you do have! Mix and match. For example, if your chosen dinnerware has a white interior with a colored or decorated rim, add plain white dishes for alternate guests. To stretch two placesettings into four, place a plain white salad plate on top of the dinner plate of your chosen pattern for one guest and reverse this layering (salad plate of your chosen pattern on top of plain white dinner plate) for guests in adjacent chairs. Likewise, four placesettings can be stretched into eight! Utilize the colors of your design pattern in accessories such as napkins, placemats, candles or flowers. The possibilities are indeed endless and your results will be dynamic.

Flowers... for a special occasion, place a single flower on each lady's plate (usually every other chair).

For an interesting effect, place a few assorted flowers in clean glass jars or bottles which have been washed and saved from the ingredients used in preparing the meal. For example, if you are serving a salad with vinaigrette dressing, use the olive oil or vinegar jar to hold carnations. A recycled mustard jar with small daisies is nice to accent a table when hamburgers or brats are the dinner entrée.

basics
for the kitchen

pots and pans...

While your selection of pots and pans is certainly a personal one determined by a variety of factors, a basic set of mid-to-heavy-weight stainless steel saucepans would be a good choice. Try to include 2-quart, 3-quart, 5-quart and 8-quart sizes, with one or more of these having a non-stick coating. Non-stick fry pans in varied sizes would also be very helpful.

Whichever set you choose, make sure all handles are attached securely. Nothing will spoil a party faster than having a pot full of boiling liquid break apart!

small appliances...

Can opener (electric or manual, whichever you prefer)
Portable electric mixer
Electric coffee maker
Electric slow cooker
Electric food processor and/or blender

casserole and baking dishes...

Glass baking dishes (such as Pyrex® or CorningWare®) in varied sizes are an absolute must. They are relatively inexpensive, can be used to cook or bake almost anything, and clean-up is easy in the dishwasher. Essential sizes include 1-quart (usually measuring 8"x8"), 2-quart (usually measuring 9"x9") and 3-quart (usually measuring 9"x13") shallow bakeware. The smaller pans often come with glass covers which are also invaluable. If you have been fortunate to have received beautifully decorated or painted ceramic casserole dishes, use them! Most are heartier than they look and can go from the oven to the table to the dishwasher.

bowls, boards and utensils...

Set of lightweight mixing bowls (stainless steel or glass)
Non-stick baking pans, including a fluted tube pan such as Bundt®
Pyrex® measuring cups for liquid measures
Measuring spoons and cups for dry measures
Cutting board or chopping mat
Colander
Sharp knives
Spatulas (at least one for non-stick finishes)
Long wooden spoons
Wire whisk
Potato masher

a few tips on how to...

...make delicious coffee:

Use less coffee than the coffee manufacturer suggests! For drip coffee makers, five rounded tablespoons for ten 6-ounce cups of coffee should be ample for most guests. Always start with fresh, cold water and a clean filter.

...chop onions without crying:

Remove all papery layers of onion with sharp knife; rinse well with cool water. Working quickly, cut onion into round slices; discard ends. Next, cut each slice to resemble a checkerboard, making vertical cuts and then horizontal cuts in one-half inch intervals

...eliminate pesky odors from the air:

Baking a sweet dessert will eliminate strong cooking odors. Apple pie seems to work best. Of course, you already know about lighting candles...

...eliminate pesky odors from hands:

Dip hands in milk or lemon juice or vinegar, then wash in cold water to remove smells from garlic and onion. You also might try rubbing a stainless steel spoon with your fingers under cold running water.

...prepare perfect hardboiled eggs:

Place uncooked eggs in saucepan and cover with cold water. Bring to a boil; lower heat and continue to boil gently for 10 minutes. Cover and remove from heat. When eggs are cool enough to handle, immerse in cold water, crack and roll against side of sink and peel under running cold water. The peels should slide off.

...remove wax from votive holder:

When candle is completely extinguished and cool, immerse votive in very hot soapy water for a minute or two. Using tip of blunt knife, pop out used wax and discard. Continue to wash votive holder with hot soapy water, being careful to not allow excess wax to enter sink drain.

A note on measures: when measuring ingredients for baking, use of specific measuring spoons and cups is a must for beginning bakers.

When cooking, however, personal taste is more important than the recipe amount, especially with regard to teaspoons and tablespoons. For the recipes in this book, ordinary teaspoons and tablespoons from the silverware drawer have been used to determine amounts because it is so much easier and faster.

This Guide is intended to help newlywed couples entertain friends and family... however, what about occasionally reducing these recipes by half and entertaining just each other?

brunch and lunch

Brunch and lunch... these meals are the highlight of a leisurely day. It's an especially nice way to entertain family.

The recipes included here have been selected mainly for ease of preparation. Some of the brunch recipes can be made in advance (the night before) and just popped into the oven. My favorite lunch selection is Hoagie Sandwiches, which can be completely assembled from simple ingredients purchased at the deli section and salad bar of your local grocer.

Please use your prettiest dishes and bakeware and put a few fresh flowers on the table. I'll be thinking about you as you enjoy that second cup of coffee.

cheesy egg soufflé

6 slices white bread
3 cups shredded Cheddar cheese (12 ounces)
8 eggs
3 cups milk
1/4 teaspoon salt
1/4 teaspoon white pepper

Note: You do not need to take the crust off the bread.

Serves 6 - 8

This really should be named "Easy Cheesy Egg Soufflé". It is best when put together the night before and baked right before serving.

Try using a Mexican blend of shredded cheese for a bit more zip. If you're really adventurous, try a small pinch of red cayenne pepper instead of white pepper.

1 Grease or spray 9"x13" baking dish. Layer bread in single layer on bottom; arrange cheese evenly on top of bread.

2 In separate bowl, beat all eggs well with wire whisk or electric mixer on low speed. Add all of milk, salt and pepper; continue to beat until frothy.

3 Pour milk/egg mixture on top of cheese. Press with fork to make sure all cheese is covered with liquid. Cover tightly with foil; refrigerate overnight.

4 One hour before serving: preheat oven to 325°. Remove foil; bake uncovered for one hour. Serve immediately.

Orange juice, melon wedges and heat-and-eat mini-sausages make this Cheesy Egg Soufflé complete.

Using package directions as your guide to heating sausages, perhaps you can use your oven for double duty. If sausage directions ask for higher oven temperature, maintain 325° but increase time accordingly. Sausages will still be delicious and everything will be hot at the same time.

sausage biscuits

1 pound sausage

1 can buttermilk biscuits, flaky layer style (10 ounces)

1/2 cup shredded Cheddar cheese

Makes 20 biscuits

Sausage biscuits are a good choice for an easy breakfast or brunch when lots of guests are expected. Serve with juice and fresh fruit in season.

Please experiment with different varieties of sausage. There are some excellent Italian blends available.

1. Preheat oven to 400°.
2. With sharp knife, remove any casings from sausage. Fry until browned and crumbly. Use fork to mash and separate meat. Drain.
3. Using fingers, separate each biscuit into 2 halves. Place on ungreased non-stick baking sheet, sides touching. Press cooked sausage onto each biscuit; sprinkle cheese on top.
4. Bake for 10 - 12 minutes. Biscuits should be lightly browned on bottom and flaky on top. Serve immediately.

up late the night before and you don't want to cook...

Sliced bagels and cream cheese, assorted fruits and orange juice make a terrific brunch.

Make a pot of fresh coffee and have a variety of tea bags available.

prepare ahead

french toast

1 loaf French or Italian bread
1/2 cup butter (1 stick), softened
3/4 cup sugar
6 eggs
2 cups milk
1/4 teaspoon salt
Cinnamon

Serves 6

For European flair, serve with lemon wedges and powdered sugar.

For traditional French toast lovers, pass maple syrup and different flavored jellies.

To be really elegant, place a small cluster of fresh grapes or kiwi slices on each plate.

1 The night before serving, grease or spray 9"x13" baking dish. Cut bread into one-inch slices; place closely together in single layer on bottom of dish. (You probably won't need entire loaf.)

2 In separate bowl, use electric mixer to combine softened butter and sugar. Add eggs, milk and salt; continue to beat until eggs are well mixed.

3 Pour milk/egg mixture on top of bread, making sure all slices are well soaked with liquid. Use spoon to cover edges of bread. Press butter particles evenly into all slices; sprinkle with cinnamon. Cover tightly with foil; refrigerate overnight.

4 Forty-five minutes before serving: preheat oven to 325°. Remove foil; bake uncovered for 45 minutes.

5 Transfer slices to serving plate. Serve with lemon wedges and powdered sugar and/or flavored syrups and jellies.

ham and cheese croissants

6 croissant rolls

1 pound deli ham, sliced
1/2 pound Monterey Jack cheese, sliced
Honey mustard

Garnish: lettuce, tomatoes, pickles

Serves 4 - 6

1 Slice croissant rolls in half, horizontally. Spread both halves with honey mustard.

2 Layer ham and cheese; replace top half of croissants.

3 If you prefer these sandwiches hot, wrap prepared croissants in foil and heat in hot oven (400°) for about 5 minutes before serving.

4 Garnish each plate with lettuce, tomatoes and pickles, if desired.

Monterey Jack cheese is a specialty in Monterey County, California, where it was first made. This semi-soft, mild cheese can be found in the deli department of most grocers.

These sandwiches can be made in advance, wrapped individually in foil and kept in the refrigerator for several hours until ready to serve.

hoagie sandwiches

1 or 2 loaves Italian bread
Sliced deli meats and cheeses
Lettuce
Sliced tomatoes
Sliced onions
Pickles
Olives
Mayonaise
Mustard
Oil and vinegar

1 Prepare bread by slicing horizontally lengthwise (one long slice).

2 Layer various fillings between bread halves; spread with condiments.

3 Slice sandwich into individual servings approximately 3 inches wide; arrange on a large platter. Garnish with lettuce and additional pickles or olives.

This is so simple you are probably wondering why it deserves space in a cookbook... but then this not primarily a cookbook. Remember... it is a guide to entertaining and it is intended to be simple! If you are really short on time, buy all ingredients at the salad bar and just assemble when you are ready.

Serve with cole slaw or potato salad, also purchased from the deli section of your grocery. Add chips and cold drinks. How about a bag of whole baby carrots?

Instead of deli meat, you might like to include tuna salad. You could either buy this at the deli, or make your own:

Combine one large can tuna, drained, with a few tablespoons of mayonaise and pickle relish, to taste. Lettuce, tomatoes, onions, pickles and mild white cheese go well with tuna.

bacon, cheddar and tomato

French or Italian bread
(enough for 12 slices)

1 pound bacon
Cheddar cheese, unsliced (6 ounces)
3 - 4 tomatoes
Coarse ground black pepper
Mayonaise

Serves 4 - 6

1 Using large skillet, fry bacon slices until crisp. Drain on paper towels. Sprinkle pepper to taste.

2 Using a cheese slicer or very sharp knife, slice cheese very thinly. Slice tomatoes diagonally.

3 Slice bread in thick diagonal slices; spread each slice with mayonaise. Sprinkle with coarse black pepper. Layer with bacon, tomatoes and cheese. Top with second piece of bread. Use any extra bacon as garnish.

4 Optional: Fry bacon; slice cheese and tomatoes in advance. Cover and keep chilled until ready to serve. Make sandwiches immediately before serving.

These sandwiches are good anytime, but if you have access to homegrown tomatoes, they are outstanding. In the absence of homegrown tomatoes, I prefer the Roma variety.

I can't tell you exactly how much bread to buy, since all loaves are so varied in size; just make sure the loaf is large enough to have 12 thick slices. If the baguette is particularly small or thin, buy two.

for unexpected guests...

keep a few boxes of macaroni and cheese in the cupboard to serve with a package of hot dogs from the freezer. With buns and chips, you've got a meal.

down under pizza

1 ready-to-bake pizza crust **(10 - 12 inches)**

1 cup pizza sauce
2 cups shredded mozzarella cheese
1 cup crushed pineapple
1/4 pound deli ham

Serves 4

1 Preheat oven to 450°.

2 Spread pizza sauce onto pizza crust, being careful to not spread too close to the edge to prevent spills in the oven. Cover with mozzarella cheese.

3 Drain crushed pineapple well; place on top of cheese. Slice ham into thin strips; arrange on top of pineapple.

4 Place directly on center rack in preheated oven. Bake 10 - 12 minutes, or until pizza crust is crisp and cheese is bubbly.

This actually should be called Hawaiian Pizza, since it originates from the islands of Hawaii. I call it Down Under Pizza since it originated in our home when my daughter Pamela went to Australia and lived on it for six months.

The amounts of all ingredients are just approximate... add more (or less) of anything listed. If you don't have pizza sauce, use spaghetti sauce.

three cheese
pizza

1 ready-to-bake pizza crust **(10 - 12 inches)**

1 cup ricotta cheese
1/2 cup Blue cheese, crumbled
1 cup shredded mozzarella cheese
1/4 cup roasted peppers, sliced
1/4 cup black olives, sliced

Serves 4

1 Preheat oven to 450°.

2 Combine ricotta cheese with crumbled Blue cheese; spread onto pizza crust. Cover with mozzarella cheese.

3 Arrange sliced roasted peppers and olives decoratively on top.

4 Place directly on center rack in preheated oven. Bake 10 - 12 minutes or until pizza crust is crisp and cheese is bubbly.

I am including this colorful recipe because it is a different type of pizza - no tomato sauce. It is nice with a salad for lunch... or cut into very thin slices as an appetizer before dinner.

A pizza stone is very helpful to keep the pizza warm and crisp. The stone should be preheated, if used.

first dinner party

The first time for anything is sometimes awkward, sometimes humorous and always memorable. So it will be the first time you host a dinner party. The first time I entertained as a new bride I served very small green peas with a huge soup ladle. It was all I had. My guests are laughing about it to this day... more than thirty years later. If a dinner party can be remembered for thirty years, I would say it was a huge success. Another time, after I had been married for fifteen years and had a little more experience with entertaining, I was attempting to roast a fillet of beef in a new oven which had a broken temperature gauge (that of course I didn't know about). The beef wouldn't cook so I kept serving wine to a houseful of new neighbors that were meeting for the first time. Two hours (and many bottles of wine) later when we finally sat down to eat, no one cared how the meal tasted and by then the new neighbors were all good friends.

To make your first time easier I am taking a suggestion from a young bride in Indiana named Emily who tells me that she always serves guests spaghetti and meat sauce because that is all she knows how to cook. Wonderful! Everybody likes spaghetti and meat sauce. I have only one suggestion for you and Emily to make this meal a little more elegant... Instead of the usual garnish of grated Parmesan cheese that comes from a can, purchase a small container of fresh grated or shredded Parmesan cheese usually found in the dairy section of your local grocer. This one little change will make quite a big difference.

spaghetti with meat sauce

1 pound ground beef
1 jar or can spaghetti sauce (26 ounces)
1 package spaghetti (12 ounces)

Optional garnish:
Fresh grated or shredded Parmesan cheese

Serves 4

1 Crumble ground beef into a 3-quart saucepan. Cook over medium heat, uncovered, until meat begins to brown. Mash with fork to separate; turn with spatula as needed to brown all meat evenly. Drain fat.

2 Add spaghetti sauce to browned meat. Simmer over low heat, stirring occasionally, for approximately 5 minutes until sauce is very hot and begins to bubble. Lower heat; cover to prevent spattering on stove. Do not boil.

3 Prepare pasta according to package directions. Rinse with hot water and drain.

4 To serve, place drained pasta in large bowl and spoon hot meatsauce on top. Pass fresh grated cheese for guests to serve themselves.

Perfect for your "first time" dinner! Remember the fresh grated or shredded Parmesan cheese from the dairy department.

Serve with salad from the grocer's salad bar, cookies and ice cream for dessert, and your dinner will be a huge success.

Now you're ready for a few more recipes, along with some simple hints and instructions. Just try one or two things at a time.

The most important ingredient is a sense of humor. Innocent goofs will make the party that much more fun. Too much salt or burned vegetables will guarantee you and your guests something to joke about during dinner and for years to come. I promise.

the main event

The main dinner. Sounds formidable. The mission of this Guide is to make it easy.

Once you get a knack for entertaining, you will be the most popular couple in your group. You will have a couple over, then they will reciprocate. When they come to your home, they will be happy to help out by bringing something. Likewise, you will take something when you go to their home. On and on... Everyone participates, everyone has fun. No one couple has to bear all of the effort or all of the expense. For most of the recipes included in this Guide, the hardest part is assembling the ingredients. Cooking is the easy part.

In the beginning, entertaining might seem expensive as you have to collect ingredients for the first time, but before you know it, you will have a pantry well-stocked with basics. And, a calendar well-scribbled with invitations and party plans.

drinks and appetizers

Drinks have the ability to set the stage for the party. Whatever the time of day, people almost always seem to arrive thirsty. Alcoholic and non-alcoholic drinks are included here for your guests' pleasure.

This author hates to be an advocate of alcohol (please do not allow guests to drive home if noticeably influenced by alcohol!!), but unless your guests are teetotalers, a little 'spirit' can enliven the party. Certainly a bottle of wine or mixed drinks would be a nice option. There are no suggestions of which wine to drink with any particular dinner; rather this is left to the gourmet magazines. But, it would be nice to usually have a bottle of red wine and a bottle of white wine available. (Again in this author's experience the cost or brand of wine is not particularly important; you are entertaining friends or family, not the royalty of England.) In addition, offering a variety of soft drinks and beer are appreciated. Oh yes... Water! Bottled or in a pitcher, water is a must.

Necessity and nicety aside... the act of offering drinks gives the host and hostess an easy way to greet newcomers and make initial conversation.

dai'-qui/ri n.

a cocktail made of rum, sugar and lime or lemon juice

Reference: Webster's New World Dictionary of American English, Third College Edition, Copyright © 1988 by Simon & Schuster, Inc. NY

watermelon daiquiries

1/2 medium watermelon, seedless
1/2 cup sugar
1-1/2 cups light rum

1 lime, sliced, for garnish

Serves 4 - 6
(Makes approximately 2 quarts)

1 Remove all rind from watermelon; cut fruit into chunks.

2 In electric blender or food processor fitted with metal mixing blade, process fruit until liquid. (May have to do this in small batches.) Add sugar and rum, and mix well.

3 Pour into plastic or glass container; cover and freeze for approximately 6 hours or more. (Drink should be neither liquid or solid, but slushy.)

4 When ready to serve, pour into stemmed glasses. Garnish with half-slices of lime placed on rim of glass.

This can be made in advance and stored, covered, in the freezer for several days.

It is a particularly good drink to serve at a summer barbeque.

Did you ask for a blender?
Did you get one?

If so, these drink recipes will
help you to use it.

strawberry margaritas

1 can frozen limeade concentrate (6 ounces)
1 package frozen strawberries (16 ounces)
2 handfuls ice cubes
1 cup cold water
1/2 cup sugar
1 cup tequila

Optional: course salt to frost rims; lime cut in wedges for garnish

Serves 4 - 6
(Makes approximately 2 quarts)

1 Thaw strawberries slightly.

2 In electric blender, process all ingredients until slushy. (You will probably have to do this in small batches.)

3 Combine all puréed ingredients together in large pitcher. Mix well.

4 If desired, wipe the rims of the empty glasses with lime wedge, then dip into salt. Garnish with lime wedges placed on rim of glass.

A traditional margarita includes a small amount of Triple Sec liqueur, which you may certainly wish to add. I have not included it here only to attempt to minimize the ingredient list.

If frozen strawberries have been pre-sweetened, eliminate some or all of the added sugar.

sparkling ice cream

1/2 gallon vanilla ice cream
2 cups sparkling wine

Optional: ground nutmeg for garnish

Serves 6 - 8
(Makes approximately 2 quarts)

1 Blend part of the softened ice cream with part of the sparkling wine in blender or food processor. Continue in batches until all of ice cream and wine are combined.

2 Serve in chilled wine or champagne glasses. If desired, garnish with a sprinkle of nutmeg in each glass when served.

Cold and creamy, this drink is certain to make any occasion more festive.

For a non-alcoholic drink, substitute a lemon-lime soda or orange juice for the sparkling wine. If using soda or orange juice, omit the nutmeg.

orange spritzer

1/2 gallon orange juice, chilled
1 liter white wine or ginger ale

Optional: lemon or lime slices or maraschino cherries for garnish

Serves 10 - 12
(Makes approximately 3 quarts)

1 Blend orange juice and wine or ginger ale in large pitcher (might have to do this in batches).

2 Serve over ice in chilled goblets. If desired, garnish with lemon or lime slices or maraschino cherries in each glass.

This is so simple you may have already thought of it!

If you are celebrating something very special, substitute an inexpensive champagne for the wine or ginger ale. Use your blender to make crushed ice.

Appetizers can be an important prelude to dinner or be served instead of a main meal. If there is no formal dinner to follow, have a variety of snacks to choose from, including some vegetarian, and have plenty! Grazing is perfect when the main event is a sports program on television or a large get-together of different groups of people.

Again, I remind you to have lots of napkins and enough small paper plates for continual refills.

sweet and hot dipping sauce

1/3 cup sherry wine
1/3 cup soy sauce
1/3 cup honey
1/4 teaspoon ground red (cayenne) pepper

Note: Red pepper is hot! You might want to start with 1/8 teaspoon.

Makes 1 cup sauce

1 Combine all ingredients in small saucepan on stovetop over low heat. Mix well with wire whisk to prevent honey from sticking to bottom of pan.

2 Continue to cook over low heat until sauce is hot and all ingredients are very well blended.

3 Transfer to serving bowl. Have available a serving spoon and small individual plates.

There is a very large variety of pre-made frozen appetizers available in regular groceries and large discount stores. Examples are egg rolls, Oriental potstickers, and frozen shrimp (breaded and non-breaded). New varieties are continually being introduced for your ease in entertaining. Take advantage!

This dipping sauce will make your appetizer extra-special.

pimento pinwheels

1 package 8" flour tortillas (soft)
1 container pimento spread (14 ounces)
1 small can black olives, chopped

Garnish: marinated olives

Makes 8 pieces per tortilla

1. Mix chopped black olives into pimento spread (according to your personal taste, you might not want to use the whole can).

2. Spread mixture on tortillas, "pizza" style, using approximately 2 - 3 tablespoons of pimento for each tortilla. Form into roll, "jelly-roll" style.

3. Slice into pinwheels. Each rolled tortilla makes about 8 pieces.

4. Arrange on serving plate; garnish with marinated olives.

Pretty to look at, easy to make, and so good to eat! Pimento Pinwheels with a garnish of whole marinated olives are an excellent accompaniment to drinks before dinner.

The tortillas and pimento spread are most likely available in refrigerated cases near the dairy department of your local grocer. Marinated olives can be bought by the jar (near the pickles) or by the pound at the deli department.

deviled eggs

6 hard boiled eggs, cooled
2 tablespoons mayonaise
1 teaspoon prepared mustard
Salt and white pepper
Paprika

Makes 12 appetizers

This is a favorite for the guys. These deviled eggs will be devoured as soon as the plate is set down.

The first time you make these eggs, they might be messy. Be patient... it gets easier with practice.

1 Slice cooked eggs in half lengthwise; remove yolks to a mixing bowl and mash well with fork.

2 Add mayonaise, mustard, sprinkle of salt and white pepper; continuing to mash with fork until all ingredients are blended and smooth. It may be necessary to add more mayonaise.

3 Spoon mixture into reserved eggwhite halves. Sprinkle with paprika.

hot pepper preserves with cream cheese

1 package cream cheese (8 ounces)
1 cup apricot preserves
1/4 teaspoon ground red (cayenne) pepper

Optional: slivered almonds for garnish

Crackers for serving

You can buy hot pepper jelly at most gourmet grocers, but it is quite a bit more expensive than making your own.

Experiment with orange marmalade or raspberry preserves. Actually, any flavor of marmalade or preserves that you like will work just fine.

1 Soften cream cheese; spread "pizza" style on serving plate.

2 In separate bowl, mix preserves with ground red pepper. Start with 1/4 teaspoon and sparingly add more if you like a hotter taste.

3 Spoon preserves onto cream cheese to cover.

4 Optional: Sprinkle with slivered almonds.

crab cocktail
with cream cheese

1 package cream cheese (8 ounces)
1/2 cup cocktail sauce
1 can lump crabmeat (6 ounces)

Optional: sliced lemon for garnish

Crackers for serving

1 Soften cream cheese. Place on serving plate; flatten slightly with back of fork.

2 Spread cocktail sauce on top of cream cheese. Drain crabmeat well; place this on top of sauce.

3 Optional: Arrange thinly sliced lemon on sides of plate, for garnish.

For variation, substitute one cup baby shrimp for the crabmeat. To maximize flavor, I would suggest using fully cooked and cleaned fresh or frozen shrimp instead of canned.

Chili sauce, found in the ketchup aisle, can be used instead of cocktail sauce.

baked brie with bourbon glaze

Brie cheese (5 - 10 ounces)
1/3 cup brown sugar
1 tablespoon bourbon
1/4 cup pecans, chopped

Flatbread crackers for serving

1 Preheat oven to 400°.

2 Slice top and side rind off cheese. Place on ovenproof serving dish.

3 Combine brown sugar with bourbon to make a paste. Spread mixture on cheese. Sprinkle pecan pieces on top.

4 Bake for about 5 minutes; or until brown sugar is melted and cheese is heated through.

5 Serve hot, with flatbread crackers.

This is a recipe that I hope you will use for many years. Its simplicity adds to its elegance.

Flatbread crackers are sometimes called crackerbread. If you can't find them, don't worry... any cracker you like will be just fine.

**a cheese slicer,
a chunk of your favorite cheese,
clusters of red seedless grapes,
and a pretty plate...**

the perfect last-minute appetizer.

salmon pâté

1 large can salmon (15 ounces)
1 package cream cheese (8 ounces)
1/2 teaspoon onion powder
1 lemon

Optional: parsley flakes for garnish

1 Remove bones, skin and liquid from salmon; place in workbowl of food processor, fitted with metal mixing blade.

2 Add cream cheese, juice from one-half of the lemon and onion powder. Mix until very well blended and smooth.

3 Transfer to serving bowl. Garnish with slices from the remainder of lemon, and parsley.

4 Cover and chill.

Another simple appetizer using your food processor. There is no cooking involved. In order to save time the day of the party, make this several days in advance. Keep refrigerated.

Serve with thin slices of party pumpernickel or rye bread.

antipasto platter

Assorted slices or cubes of cheese
Assorted pickles
Cherry tomatoes
Sweet peppers
Hot peppers
Pepperoni
Marinated artichokes
Marinated mushrooms
Marinated or stuffed olives

Varied servings

1 After assembling all ingredients, arrange on a serving platter. One possibility is to use a large round plate and group each ingredient as if it were a slice of pizza; place a small bowl of toothpicks in the center.

2 Cover with plastic wrap; refrigerate until ready to serve.

These ingredients are only suggestions. Feel free to add anything else you might like (or delete that which you don't like)!

Remember to put out toothpicks, napkins and small plates for guests to serve themselves.

**Please remember...
in most instances, the
amounts given are
not an absolute;
rather, just a guide.**

Cajun wings with blue cheese

10 chicken wings (split into 3 parts with tip discarded)
1 cup white wine

1/2 cup brown sugar
1/2 teaspoon red (cayenne) **pepper**
Paprika

Bottled blue cheese dressing

Makes 20 appetizers

This tastes as good as those in your favorite restaurant.

Make sure you ask the butcher to split the wings into three parts for you; discard the bony tip. If butcher can't do this, you can do it yourself with a sharp, heavy knife and a sturdy cutting board.

1 Four hours prior to serving: Rinse chicken; dry on paper towels. Combine chicken wings with wine in non-metal bowl; cover and chill.

2 Thirty minutes before serving: Preheat oven to 425°. Spray or grease baking dish.

3 In small bowl mix together brown sugar and red pepper; remove wings from wine marinade and toss with sugar mixture. Place wings in single layer in greased baking dish; sprinkle with paprika. Bake at 425°, uncovered, for 30 minutes, or until crispy.

4 Transfer to serving plate. Provide bowl of blue cheese dressing nearby.

marshmallow popcorn squares

1/2 cup butter **(1 stick)**
1 package miniature marshmallows **(10 ounces)**
8 cups popped corn
1 cup mixed nuts
2 cups M&M's® chocolate candies

Makes approximate 60 squares

1 Spray or grease 2-quart gelatin mold or cake pan.

2 Using large non-stick saucepan, melt butter over medium heat. Add marshmallows; continue to heat, stirring with wooden spoon, until all of mixture is melted.

3 Remove from heat. Add popped corn and nuts; stir to combine. Mix in chocolate candies. Press into greased pan. Cover with plastic wrap.

4 Chill at least 2 hours; remove from pan. Cut into 1-inch pieces using a sharp, heavy knife.

Sticky and gooey, but irresistable. Be prepared to lick your fingers.

If you want this treat less gooey, add a few more cups of popped corn. Work fast, before the melted marshmallows cool and harden.

Be sure to check out the chapters on "Three Ingredients or Less" and "What a Crock" to see more ideas for Appetizers.

soups and salads

Soups and salads can either be part of the main dinner, generally as a first course, or.... can be the dinner. The recipes in this chapter actually go well paired together to make a wonderful casual meal. When soup and/or salad will be the main event, just make the portions larger and accompany with a special bread, such as focaccia. The soup recipes here can be made in advance and kept chilled in the refrigerator for a day or two. Simply re-heat when ready to serve.

Another reminder: if you make the soup and salad, have guests bring the dessert. If soup is to be followed by an entrée, choose something simple like Marinated Pork Chops with Garlic and ask your guests to bring everything else!

soups ...

cream of tomato soup with basil

2 cans condensed tomato soup
(10-3/4 ounces each)

1 can light cream
1 can milk
1 teaspoon dried basil

Garnish: additional basil

Serves 4

You never knew soup could be so simple.

This is a good choice for lunch when you don't have much time to be in the kitchen. Serve with sandwiches made with thick Italian bread.

1 Combine all ingredients in a 3-quart saucepan. Using low to medium heat, cook for 5 minutes, stirring occasionally. Do not boil.

2 If desired, garnish with additional basil on each serving.

corn chowder

1/2 cup butter (1 stick)
1/3 cup quick-mixing flour (such as Wondra®)
1 can chicken broth (14 ounces)
2 cans corn kernels (15 ounces each)
1 can creamed corn (15 ounces)
2 cups light cream
1 teaspoon salt
1 teaspoon white pepper

Optional: 2 cups cooked ham, cubed, or 2 cups polish sausage, sliced

Optional garnish: paprika

Serves 6

Lots of ingredients, but oh-so-easy! Just be sure to open all the cans before you start. That is truly the hardest part.

If being served as a main entrée, the addition of ham or polish sausage definitely makes the chowder more complete. Warm focaccia bread, salad and wine are ideal accompaniments.

1 Drain corn kernels and purée briefly in food processor.

2 Melt butter in large soup pot; stir in flour with wire whisk. Add chicken broth, mixing continually, scraping sides and bottom of pot as needed to keep flour from sticking. Heat until almost boiling and liquid starts to thicken.

3 Add puréed corn, creamed corn, light cream, salt and white pepper. If including cooked ham or polish sausage, add this now also.

4 Continue to simmer over medium heat for about 10 minutes, stirring occasionally. Do not allow to boil. Optional: If not including ham or sausage, sprinkle paprika on each serving for garnish.

pu-rée v.

a thick, moist, smooth-textured form of cooked vegetables, fruits, etc., usually made by pressing the pulp through a sieve or by whipping it in a blender or food processor

Reference: Webster's New World Dictionary of American English, Third College Edition, Copyright © 1988 by Simon & Schuster, Inc. NY

cheddar broccoli chowder

1/2 cup butter (1 stick)
1/3 cup quick-mixing flour (such as Wondra®)
1 can chicken broth (14 ounces)
1 can cheddar cheese soup (10-3/4 ounces)
2 cups milk
2 cups light cream
1 package frozen chopped broccoli (16 ounces)
1 teaspoon salt
1/2 teaspoon white pepper

Garnish:
1 cup shredded cheddar cheese

Serves 4 - 6

1 Using medium heat, melt butter in very large pot; stir in flour with wire whisk. Add chicken broth, mixing continually, scraping sides and bottom of pot as needed to keep flour from sticking. Heat until almost boiling and liquid starts to thicken.

2 Add milk, light cream, cheese soup, chopped broccoli, salt and white pepper, continuing to stir and scrape bottom of pan. Cook over medium heat for about 5 minutes. Lower heat if soup starts to boil.

3 Garnish each bowl with several tablespoons of shredded cheddar cheese.

This is made so fast! Have your cans opened and ingredients measured before you start.

This soup generously feeds four persons as a main entrée or six persons as an accompaniment to something light such as sandwiches for lunch.

Note: If you are using a pot with a non-stick finish, be sure to use wooden or plastic spoons and spatulas. Metal will scratch.

vegetarian chili

2 cans kidney or pinto beans (15 ounces each)
2 cans diced tomatoes (14 ounces each)
1 package chili seasoning (1 ounce)
1/2 teaspoon onion powder

Optional garnish: shredded cheddar cheese

Serves 4 - 6

1 Drain beans; place in 3-quart saucepan. Add tomatoes, chili seasoning and onion powder; stir to combine. Simmer over medium heat for approximately 10 minutes.

2 Optional: Provide shredded cheddar cheese in nearby bowl for guests to help themselves.

For your guests who might not be vegetarian, serve this hot and spicy chili with hot dogs as you watch your favorite football game. It can be made in advance and kept warm on the stove for hours. Set out plates and all the fiixins' for guests to help themselves.

This recipe is for a small group; for a large gathering, see the section on Chili Plus in the chapter on Party Themes.

Once you realize how easy and inexpensive soups and salads are for entertaining, you will have this combination often. If you want a bit more food, have extra appetizers.

If you are inviting one other couple, ask them to bring the salad, and buy cookies and ice cream for dessert. If two other couples are invited, hosts provide soup, one guest couple prepares salad, and the other supplies dessert. Hosts decide who brings what. Don't forget the wine and hot bread and candles for ambiance.

vegetable beef soup

1 pound ground beef
1/2 cup butter (1 stick)
1 cup quick-mixing flour (such as Wondra®)
4 tablespoons beef bouillon
8 cups hot water
1 package mixed vegetables, frozen (16 ounces)
1 can pinto beans, drained (15 ounces)
1 can diced tomatoes (14 ounces)
1 teaspoon salt
1 teaspoon pepper

Serves 8 - 10

Another recipe that is a favorite of bride and groom, Vicki and Andrew. An old favorite, still simple and good, they serve it often when they entertain.

Hot garlic bread and red wine are natural accompaniments.

1 Using large soup pot (8-quart or larger), melt butter; stir in flour with wire whisk to make paste. Add hot water and bouillon slowly, stirring and scraping bottom of pot to prevent flour from sticking. Continue to cook over medium heat.

2 Add vegetables, drained beans, tomatoes, salt and pepper; stir well to mix. Adjust heat so that soup simmers; do not allow to boil.

3 In separate fry pan, brown ground beef until crumbly; drain fat. Add meat to soup. Simmer over low heat for 2 hours, stirring occasionally.

If, as brand-new newlyweds, you are reluctant to try this recipe for French Onion Soup... please consider it at a later date. The author made gallons of it attempting to make it as simple and delicious as possible.

Guaranteed, it can be mastered with ease after you have assembled all of the ingredients. While the onions are frying, pour yourselves a glass of the wine you are using to sip as you stir. Measure out the broth and tidy up the kitchen.

french onion soup

4 large onions (yellow)
1/2 cup olive oil
2 tablespoons sugar
Salt and pepper

1/4 cup quick-mixing flour
(such as Wondra®)
4 cups beef broth
1 cup wine

Shredded mozzarella cheese
Croutons

Serves 6 - 8

The beef broth can be canned or made by adding 4 teaspoons beef bouillon (or beef soup base) to 4 cups of very hot water. If you want more highly flavored broth, add an extra teaspoon of bouillon. The wine can be any kind you like, other than sparkling.

This rich soup makes a great main entrée with large green salad and cheesy garlic bread.

1 Using a large, deep saucepan (5-quart or larger), heat oil. Add sugar and several sprinkles of salt and pepper; stir with wooden spoon.

2 While oil is heating, peel and slice onions very thin. (If you have a food processor, use the slicing blade to do this quickly.) Add onions to saucepan and sauté over medium heat until onions are limp and glossy, about 15 minutes. Stir as needed.

3 Lower heat, and thoroughly mix in flour. Add beef broth and wine and mix together, scraping sides and bottom to keep flour from sticking.

4 Cover and simmer over very low heat for about one hour. Check occasionally to make sure mixture is "bubbling", not boiling. Adjust seasonings; might need more pepper.

5 When ready to serve, ladle into large bowls; top with croutons and shredded cheese.

salads...

Crisp lettuce, ripe tomatoes and dressing... combine these three ingredients and you will have salad. Add a few sliced vegetables, grated cheese, crumbled bacon or croutons... and you can have salad extraordinaire.

Most people like an oil and vinegar vinaigrette dressing, but experiment with different kinds. Ranch and poppy seed are also quite popular. For greatest ease, use some of the excellent salad dressings available already bottled. If you are adventuresome, fresh vinaigrettes are quite easy to make (recipe follows).

Salads are basically failproof. Add whichever vegetables, meats or cheeses that you like. And of course, the recipes here list only a few of the many endless possibilities... I know you will develop your own favorites to include.

How to remove core and cut iceberg lettuce for salads: Remove any wilted leaves on outside of lettuce. Holding the top of rounded head in both hands, bottom of lettuce (core) facing down, smash hard on counter. Core can now easily be taken out. Rinse whole lettuce under cool running water and wrap in cloth or paper towels to dry. Using the same technique for slicing an onion, slice whole lettuce vertically in one-inch widths, then re-slice each of these sections horizontally. This should result in perfect cut lettuce for salad.

Contrary to what you might have been told, all lettuce can be cut rather than needing to be torn. It's much faster. If done in advance, cover with damp towel and refrigerate.

the basic salad

One head lettuce
2 cups cherry tomatoes
Seasoned salt and pepper

Bottled dressing

Optional: seasoned croutons, sliced carrots, red onions or cucumbers, and/or shredded cheese

Serves 4 - 6

1 Rinse lettuce and tomatoes with cool water. Set on cloth or paper towels to drain and dry.

2 If using iceberg lettuce, remove core and cut into bite-size pieces. If using other varieties of lettuce, such as romaine, simply cut into bite-size pieces, discarding end piece.

3 In large bowl, mix cut lettuce with tomatoes and any other optional ingredients. Sprinkle seasoned salt and pepper to taste. Transfer to serving bowl; refrigerate until ready to serve.

4 Note: If pre-mixing dressing with other salad ingredients, toss right before serving to prevent salad from becoming soggy.

One head of lettuce usually serves 4 - 6 people, but you might want to buy more if salad is the main dish. It is fun to mix different varieties of lettuce.

For optimum flavor, it is best to toss vinaigrette, ranch or poppy seed dressings with other salad ingredients prior to serving; for thicker salad dressings, such as Thousand Island and blue cheese, it is probably best to serve these dressings separately in a small bowl for guests to help themselves.

balsamic vinaigrette

1 cup olive oil
1/2 cup balsamic vinegar
1 teaspoon Dijon mustard
1/4 teaspoon garlic powder
1/4 teaspoon salt
1/4 teaspoon black pepper

Makes approximately 1-1/2 cups vinaigrette

1 In small bowl, combine oil, vinegar, mustard, and all seasonings. Mix well with fork or wire whisk. (Or... put all ingredients in small jar with tight fitting lid and shake to combine.)

2 Cover; keep chilled until ready to serve.

Balsamic vinaigrette is classic. It should stay fresh for several days if stored tightly covered in the refrigerator.

If you want a lighter, sweeter vinaigrette, substitute rice vinegar for the balsamic vinegar.

romaine with pecans and vinaigrette

1/2 cup Vinaigrette (preceding page)

1 large head romaine lettuce
1 can mandarin oranges (11 ounces)
1/2 cup pecan halves
1 small red onion
Salt and black pepper, to taste

Serves 4 - 6

1 Rinse lettuce with cool water; set on cloth or paper towels to drain. When dry, cut into bite-size pieces, discarding end piece. Drain mandarin oranges; slice red onion very thin.

2 Combine cut lettuce, orange segments, pecan halves, and sliced onion in large bowl. Cover and chill.

3 When ready to serve, add vinaigrette; toss to combine. Sprinkle with salt and pepper. Transfer to serving bowl; serve immediately.

This salad is sweet and pungent at the same time. I predict it will soon be one of your favorites, as it is mine.

In summer, I substitute ripe strawberries, sliced, for the mandarin oranges. To make this salad a complete meal, add strips of sautéed chicken. Fabulous!

layered salad

One large head iceburg lettuce
1 small red onion
1 cup green peas, frozen
1 cup cheddar cheese, shredded
1/2 cup bacon pieces
2 eggs, hard-boiled
1 cup mayonaise

Serves 6

1 Rinse lettuce with cool water; drain on paper towels. Remove core and cut into bite-size pieces. Slice red onion very thin; cut each slice in half. Cook peas briefly; drain. (Overcooking will cause peas to become mushy.) Slice hard-boiled eggs.

2 Place 1/2 of lettuce into bottom of large salad bowl. Layer sliced onion, peas, shredded cheese, bacon pieces, and sliced eggs. Place remaining lettuce on top.

3 Spread mayonaise on top. Cover and refrigerate until ready to serve.

4 When ready to serve, toss all ingredients to mix.

This delicious salad is even better if put together the day before. Toss immediately before serving.

Use your judgement and personal taste preferences regarding amounts. You might not want to use the entire red onion; or you might want to add a little extra shredded cheese. The important tip for this salad is to use a good quality mayonaise.

Bacon pieces are found near the spices at your grocer.

greek salad with feta cheese and lemon

One large head romaine lettuce
1 cup cherry tomatoes
1 small red onion
1/2 cup feta cheese, crumbled
1/4 cup olive oil
1/4 cup lemon juice
1 tablespoon dried oregano
Salt and black pepper, to taste

Serves 4 - 6

I apologize for giving you a recipe with so many ingredients. You might save this for a night when all you have to make is the salad.

Feta cheese can be found already crumbled in the dairy department. I suggest buying the less expensive variety.

1 Rinse lettuce and tomatoes with cool water; set on cloth or paper towels to drain. When lettuce is dry, cut into bite-size pieces, discarding end piece. Slice red onion thinly.

2 Combine cut lettuce, tomatoes, sliced onion, and crumbled cheese in large bowl. Cover and chill.

3 When ready to serve, add olive oil, lemon juice, oregano, salt and pepper; toss to combine. Transfer to serving bowl; serve immediately.

entrées

The entrée is the main part of your dinner. Often it is the only thing you will have to actually prepare; the other parts can either be purchased or brought by your guests. Some of the following recipes are very easy with simple ingredients, while others might require a little more assembling. All included, however are definitely do-able. The important thing is to try! Do it together, with a sense of humor (does it really matter if the spaghetti is limp?), and don't worry about a mistake or two. I am beginning this chapter with more variations on pasta since that is what so many of you have told me you like to make.

When you first start entertaining, keep your parties small to lessen the preparation and the expense.

marinara with penne

2 jars or cans spaghetti sauce (26 ounces each)
1 can tomato paste (6 ounces)
2 teaspoons Italian seasoning, dried
1 teaspoon sugar
1/2 teaspoon garlic powder

16 ounces penne pasta

Optional garnish: fresh parsley
Fresh grated Parmesan cheese

Serves 6 - 8

Note: If you are using a particularly thick or chunky bottle of spaghetti sauce (or if you want a thinner sauce) you can omit all or part of the tomato paste.

Tastes like "made from scratch".

While you can use dried grated cheese and parsley from a spice bottle and it will still be delicious, having fresh garnish truly makes this simple dinner elegant and memorable.

Please experiment with different sizes and shapes of pasta. The selections are endless. Penne is a short, tubular variety (as is rigatoni), but shells and spirals are also fun.

1 Combine the spaghetti sauce, tomato paste, Italian seasoning, sugar and garlic in a 3-quart saucepan. Simmer over low heat, stirring occasionally, for approximately 5 minutes until sauce is very hot and beginning to bubble. Do not boil.

2 While sauce is heating, prepare pasta according to package directions; drain. Rinse with hot water.

3 To serve, place drained pasta in large bowl and spoon hot sauce on top. With kitchen shears, snip fresh parsley onto sauce. Pass fresh grated cheese for guests to serve themselves.

meatballs and marinara

One recipe Marinara with Penne
(as prepared on previous page)

2 pounds ground beef
1/2 cup seasoned bread crumbs
2 eggs
1 tablespoon Italian seasoning, dried

Optional garnish:
Fresh grated Parmesan cheese

Serves 6 - 8

For ambitious couples, I am including this meatball recipe for pasta and meatballs. For those wanting an easier way, simply buy two pounds of Italian meatballs frozen and add to the sauce.

1 To make meatballs: Using a fork, mix eggs with bread crumbs and Italian seasoning. Using your hands, squeeze together egg/crumb mixture with ground beef until well combined. Shape into individual balls, about 1-1/2 inches in diameter.

2 Place meatballs in large fry pan in single layer; fry for several minutes using medium low heat until browned on all sides.

3 In large saucepan, heat meatballs with sauce (see preceding page) until bubbly, stirring occasionally. Reduce heat and cover, simmering for about 10 minutes until meat is thoroughly cooked.

4 Arrange pasta, meatballs and sauce in large serving bowl. Provide grated Parmesan cheese for garnish.

more marinara ...

..... For a vegetarian version, substitute 2 cups of sliced fresh mushrooms, sautéed with 1/4 cup butter, for the meatballs. Drain any excess butter before combining with the marinara sauce.

..... If you want meat sauce instead of meatballs, brown one pound of ground beef with one teaspoon of dried Italian seasoning, and a sprinkle of garlic powder. Use fork or wooden spoon to "crumble" beef as it is cooking. Drain and add to marinara sauce.

..... For a another vegetarian entrée, sauté sliced mushrooms, quartered onions and slivers of red or green peppers in a few tablespoons of olive oil. Add to marinara sauce. Serve over pasta of your choice.

and still more.

.... Scoop out part of interiors of fresh hoagie rolls and fill with sauce and meatballs and you will have Italian meatball Grinder sandwiches. Add mozzarella cheese, if you want a richer flavor. For toasted Grinders, place filled sandwiches in shallow pan, cover loosely with foil, and heat in moderate oven (350°) for 10 minutes.

..... How about browning Italian sausage instead of traditional ground beef to add to sauce? Your grocer has many varieties to choose from. If there is "casing" on sausage, remove before browning.

.... Marinara is very, very versatile! There are no mistakes. The various directions on these pages are merely ideas. Change the ingredients and the measurements to your own tastes.

pasta with parmesan and cream

1/4 cup butter (1/2 stick)
8 ounces fresh mushrooms, rinsed and sliced

1 cup grated Parmesan cheese
1 cup heavy cream
1 cup white wine
3/4 teaspoon garlic powder
Salt and pepper

12 ounces spaghetti

Serves 4

This is a little fancier than the average pasta recipe, but worth the extra effort. A perfect meal for guests who are vegetarian.

Serve with hot Italian bread and a large green salad.

1 Using large saucepan, melt butter over medium heat. Add mushrooms; sauté for 5 minutes until they are limp and slightly darkened.

2 Add Parmesan cheese, cream, wine, and garlic powder, mixing well with wire whisk. Lower heat and continue to cook until bubbly and thickened, approximately 10 more minutes. Sprinkle with salt and pepper, to taste.

3 Cook spaghetti according to package directions, shortening cooking time suggested by a few minutes so that pasta is slightly firm (al dente). Drain.

4 Toss mushroom and cream mixture with hot, drained pasta and transfer to your prettiest oven-proof casserole dish. Cover and keep warm in low oven (275°) until ready to serve. If available, sprinkle extra Parmesan cheese and course ground black pepper on top for garnish.

sau-té' v.

to fry quickly in a pan with a little fat

Reference: Webster's New World Dictionary of American English, Third College Edition, Copyright © 1988 by Simon & Schuster, Inc. NY

If you received pasta bowls for a wedding present, get them out!

linguine with clam sauce

1 can whole clams (10 ounces)
1 can crushed tomatoes (28 ounces)
3 tablespoons parsley flakes
1/2 teaspoon garlic powder
1/4 teaspoon ground red (cayenne) pepper

Optional garnish: grated Parmesan cheese

16 ounces linguine

Serves 4

1 Add clams, including liquid, tomatoes, parsley, garlic powder and red pepper to 3-quart saucepan. Cook over medium-low heat for approximately 10 minutes, uncovered. Sauce should reduce slightly as liquid evaporates; do not boil. Adjust all seasonings.

2 In separate large saucepan, prepare linguine according to package directions. Drain. Toss hot pasta with clam sauce. Transfer to large serving bowl; serve hot.

3 Optional: Pass a small dish of grated Parmesan cheese at the table for garnish.

Be sure to buy the large, 28 ounce can of crushed tomatoes. If you can't find crushed, buy diced and drain part of the extra liquid. These tomatoes are found in the canned vegetable section of your grocer.

Have fresh foccacia bread with olive oil and herbs to pass at the table.

sundried tomatoes with **vodka** sauce

1/2 cup sundried tomatoes
(packed in olive oil)
1 tablespoon quick-mixing flour
(such as Wondra®)
1/2 teaspoon garlic powder
1 cup Parmesan cheese, grated
2 cups light cream
1/4 cup vodka

1 pound thin spaghetti or linguine

Serves 4

Just a little of this rich, flavorful sauce goes a long way.

With a simple salad and rolls, you will think you are in your favorite Italian restaurant.

1 Chop sundried tomatoes in food processor fitted with metal blade. Add flour; pulse briefly.

2 Add garlic powder and Parmesan cheese; pulse again. Add light cream and vodka and continue to blend. All tomatoes should be finely chopped.

3 Transfer to saucepan. Cook over medium heat, stirring continually and scraping bottom, just until mixture starts to boil. Lower heat, continuing to stir, and simmer slowly for about 5 minutes until mixture is reduced and slightly thickened. If mixture becomes too thick, thin with a little milk, cream or vodka; if you prefer more thickness, add a little quick-mixing flour.

4 In separate large saucepan, prepare pasta according to package directions. Drain. Toss hot pasta with sauce. Transfer to large serving bowl; serve hot.

extra easy lasagna

1 pound ground beef
1 jar or can spaghetti sauce (26 ounces)
6 uncooked lasagna noodles
2 cups ricotta cheese (15 ounces)
2 cups shredded mozzarella cheese
1/4 cup water

Serves 8

Lasagna is a treat! This version is so simple I hope you will make it often. You don't even have to boil the noodles.

Extra Easy Lasagna recipe was donated by my friend Vicki, the special new bride who inspired this book. It would make her very happy if you would all try it in her honor.

1 Preheat oven to 375°. Spray or grease a 2-quart oblong baking dish.

2 Brown beef in a large saucepan over medium-high heat. Mash with fork until crumbly. Drain fat. Add spaghetti sauce and mix to combine.

3 Spread 1-1/2 cups of the meat mixture in baking dish. Top with 3 uncooked lasagna noodles, half of the ricotta cheese and half of the mozzarella cheese. Repeat layers. Top with remaining meat mixture. (Don't worry if the layers get a little mixed up; just make sure that all noodles are covered by meat sauce.)

4 Carefully pour water around the inside edges of the baking dish. Cover tightly with foil.

5 Bake at 375° for 45 minutes. Uncover; bake 10 more minutes. Let rest 10 minutes before serving.

parmesan chicken

6 chicken breast halves, boneless, skinless

1 cup seasoned bread crumbs
1/2 cup Parmesan cheese, grated
1/2 teaspoon salt

Serves 6

If possible, slice chicken into strips while slightly frozen. Poultry, beef and fish all slice more easily when only partially thawed.

The perfect accompaniment to Parmesan Chicken is pasta with marinara sauce. For this dinner, spaghetti sauce right from the jar would be fine. Use any variety of pasta that you like.

1 Preheat oven to 400°. Spray or grease a 2-quart oblong baking dish.

2 Using large mixing bowl, combine bread crumbs, grated cheese and salt.

3 Rinse chicken under cool water; slice into strips approximately 1 inch wide. Without drying, roll each chicken piece in crumb mixture, making sure all sides are well coated. Place in greased baking dish, in single layer.

4 Bake, uncovered, in preheated oven for about 20 minutes, or until all chicken is cooked through. Outside should be golden and crisp.

lemon chicken with rosemary

1 whole chicken (3-4 pounds)
2 lemons
1/4 cup olive oil
Fresh rosemary
Garlic salt and pepper

Serves 4

1 Preheat oven to 400°. Spray or grease roasting pan. Remove loose pieces from cavity of chicken. Rinse chicken; pat dry with paper towels. Wash lemons; cut in half.

2 Using hands, rub olive oil into outside of chicken. Squeeze juice from 3 lemon halves onto chicken; put used rinds into cavity of chicken along with several sprigs rosemary. Reserve remaining rosemary and unused lemon half for garnish.

3 Place chicken in greased roasting pan, legs up. Sprinkle with garlic salt and pepper. Bake 40 minutes, uncovered. Turn chicken, legs down, sprinkle again with garlic salt and pepper; bake additional 30 - 40 minutes, uncovered, until chicken is golden.

4 Garnish with remaining lemon half, sliced, and remaining rosemary.

This is easy, delicious and looks beautiful. The lemon makes the chicken golden and crispy. Fresh rosemary can usually be found packaged in the fresh produce department of your grocer. One package is plenty.

To make this roast chicken meal complete, add a large package of frozen vegetables around chicken during the last twenty minutes of baking. Possibilities are baby carrots, green beans or green peas with onions. Vegetables will absorb the lemon and rosemary flavors and be scrumptious!

mushroom chicken with rice

3 pounds chicken, bone-in (approximately 8 pieces)
1 can cream of mushroom soup (10-3/4 ounces)
1 can French onion soup (10-3/4 ounces)
1 cup white rice, uncooked
Course ground pepper

Serves 4 - 6

This is comfort food of the highest quality. There are many variations of this recipe, but this is the easiest and the best.

Serve with your favorite wine.

1 Preheat oven to 350°.

2 Rinse chicken under cold water. Place on paper towels to drain.

3 Spray or grease a 3-quart (9"x13") casserole dish. Add uncooked rice and both cans of soup; stir with fork to mix.

4 Place chicken on top, skin side up, in single layer. Sprinkle with course ground pepper.

5 Cover tightly with foil. Bake at 350° for one hour. Uncover and continue to bake for additional 15 minutes, or until chicken is browned. Serve.

Thai ribs with bourbon

4 pounds spareribs
1/2 cup brown sugar
1/2 cup soy sauce
1/2 cup bourbon

Serves 4 - 6

1 Preheat oven to 300°. Wipe ribs with paper towels; place in large roasting pan. Combine soy sauce with bourbon.

2 With fingers or back of tablespoon, press brown sugar onto both sides of ribs. Pour sauce mixture on top of ribs. Cover pan with aluminum foil.

3 Cook for 3 hours at 300°. Remove foil covering; baste with pan juices. Continue to roast, uncovered, for an additional 30 minutes.

4 Transfer to a large platter and serve.

Note: Ribs can be prepared in advance and reheated for 30 minutes, covered, at 300°.

Takes a long time for the ribs to be tender... but so easy. This version can be made year-round in the oven. To facilitate easier cleanup of roasting pan, line with heavy aluminum foil prior to cooking.

Serve with salad, corn-on-the-cob or baked beans, and lots of paper napkins.

How much meat is the right amount to buy?

Although portions are not exact (as different people have different size appetites), in general you should allow 1/2 pound boneless meat per serving; and 3/4 pound per serving if the bone is included. All measurements are determined to be pre-cooked weight.

These amounts assume that when entertaining guests, of course it is better to have a little extra than not enough. Leftovers can always be enjoyed the next day.

marinated pork chops with garlic

2 - 3 pounds pork chops
(see Note preceding page)

1 cup red wine
1 teaspoon garlic powder
Salt and pepper

Optional: green peas, frozen (16 ounces)

Serves 4 - 6

1 At least 2 hours in advance: Rinse chops with cool water; dry on paper towels. In shallow dish, mix garlic powder with wine. Place chops in dish, coating both sides. Cover and chill.

2 When ready to serve: Place oven rack towards top of oven (about 6 - 8 inches below heating element); preheat broiler.

3 Place chops on broiler pan, single layer; sprinkle with salt and pepper. Discard marinade liquid.

4 With oven door cracked for better heat circulation, broil for about 5 - 10 minutes, depending upon thickness of chops. Turn chops over; sprinkle with salt and pepper again. Continue to broil for 5 - 7 minutes more, checking for the degree of doneness you prefer.

If you want to make a green vegetable to serve with your chops, add a package of frozen green peas to the broiler pan prior to cooking. Season and broil along with the chops.

Otherwise, sweet potatoes go well with pork. Or... stuffing prepared in 5 minutes on the stovetop. Hot rolls with butter and your meal is complete.

Cajun shrimp

1 pound shrimp,
cleaned and deveined

1 tablespoon Cajun seasoning
1 tablespoon sugar
1/4 cup lemon juice
1/4 cup soy sauce

Garnish: lemon wedges, parsley

Serves 4

1 Preheat oven to 425°. If shrimp is frozen, thaw in a bowl of cold water. Spray or grease 9"x13" baking dish.

2 Combine Cajun seasoning, sugar, lemon juice and soy sauce in mixing bowl. Add shrimp; mix to coat well. Let marinate for 15 minutes.

3 Place shrimp in greased baking dish, single layer. Bake, uncovered, at 425° for approximately 7 - 10 minutes. Shrimp is ready when it is no longer translucent and slightly browned on top.

4 Transfer to a serving platter. Garnish with lemon wedges and parsley.

Ready-to-cook shrimp can be purchased frozen, already cleaned and deveined. You have your choice of tail-on or tail removed; I prefer tail-on for a more dramatic presentation.

Fiery Cajun Shrimp is best served with a large bowl of fluffy white rice.

Be sure to check out the chapters on "Three Ingredients or Less" and "What a Crock" to see more ideas for Entrées.

accompaniments

Don't you just love the sound of the word "accompaniments"? It just kind of trills and rolls off the tongue! Much like the recipes included in the next few pages. These recipes are quick to prepare, have minimal ingredients and are almost guaranteed to please your guests.

Sometimes "accompaniments" are the focus of the meal. Delicious side dishes such as "Roast Asparagus with Bacon" or "Honey Glazed Carrots with Ginger" need only a very basic grilled meat to be complete.

An accompaniment can be as simple as having a bowl of olive oil sprinkled with herbs such as basil or thyme with hot fresh Italian bread for guests to dip into. A bottle of mixed, dried Italian seasonings is good to have on hand, if only for this purpose.

Bread is an accompaniment.

Rolls, biscuits, focaccia, Italian loaves and French baguettes, to name just a few... the selection is endless. The most important aspect of the bread you are serving is its freshness. If you have time and oven space, warmed bread or rolls are usually preferred (place in hot oven for about 10 minutes, covered with tin foil to keep it from drying out).

Pass a small bowl of butter or seasoned olive oil for guests to help themselves.

How to cook vegetables....

Most vegetables - fresh or frozen - are best cooked in a steamer basket. (If using fresh, make sure to wash, trim and/or peel appropriately before cooking.)

Place vegetables in the steamer basket inside of a saucepot. Fill pot with enough water to just barely touch the bottom of the steamer. Cover pot. Over medium heat, bring water to a boil. Lower heat slightly and continue to simmer until vegetables are heated through, but still bright in color, about 5 to 10 minutes.

If you don't have a steamer basket, immerse fresh or frozen vegetables in already boiling water. Mix in 1/2 teaspoon salt and 1 teaspoon sugar to make the vegetables more flavorful. Continue to boil, uncovered, for just a few minutes until vegetables are crisp tender but still brightly colored.

Whichever method you chose, toss hot vegetables with butter and a bit of seasoned salt and pepper and serve as soon as possible.

sautéed mushrooms
with almost anything

1 can sliced mushrooms (4 ounces)
2 tablespoons butter
Salt and pepper

Almost Anything includes (but not limited to):
Chinese pea pods, green peas, green beans, broccoli, rice and pasta

Note: You can substitute 4 ounces (1 cup) of fresh mushrooms, rinsed in bowl of cool water and drained on paper towels.

1 Melt butter in frying pan using medium-high heat. Add well-drained mushroom slices; cook until slightly darkened, about 2 or 3 minutes. Sprinkle with salt and pepper to taste.

2 Add mushrooms and butter to hot, cooked and drained vegetables, rice or pasta.

3 Toss together and serve.

What is your favorite variety of frozen vegetable? And, do you prefer white rice, brown rice or wild rice? Do you like noodles better than rice? Almost all of the above will be improved by the addition of sautéed mushrooms.

If fresh are available, by all means substitute a cup of sliced fresh mushrooms. (You will have to cook approximately 5 minutes longer and might need a little extra butter.)

Regarding amounts, a one-pound package of frozen vegetables usually serves about 4 people. One pound of pasta serves about 6 people.

spinach with cream cheese

1 package frozen chopped spinach (16 ounces)
1 package cream cheese (8 ounces)
1/4 cup butter (1/2 stick)
1 can French fried onions (15 ounces)
Salt and pepper, to taste

Serves 4 - 6

This is healthy and delicious. Did I mention easy?

This creamy accompaniment is excellent with any type of beef, pork or poultry. If you want to make in advance, complete only Steps 1 and 2, then refrigerate, covered. Do not bake until ready to serve.

1 Preheat oven to 350°. Grease or spray 2-quart casserole dish.

2 Thaw spinach; squeeze out as much excess moisture as possible. Soften cream cheese and butter by using microwave in 20 second intervals. Combine spinach, cream cheese and butter; add salt and pepper to taste. Spoon into prepared casserole dish. Arrange French fried onions on top.

3 Bake, uncovered, for 30 minutes. Serve hot.

corn with red peppers

1 can corn kernels (15 ounces)
1 can creamed corn (15 ounces)
1/4 cup roasted red peppers, sliced
2 tablespoons seasoned bread crumbs
Salt and pepper, to taste

Serves 4 - 6

Didn't I tell you accompaniments could be easy?

The roasted red peppers give this dish its pizazz. They are easily found near the pickles at your local grocer. Buy the inexpensive jar... it is just as good as the bottle with the fancier label.

The bread crumbs are a nice addition, but not as important as the roasted peppers.

1 Preheat oven to 350°. Grease or spray 2-quart casserole dish.

2 Drain corn kernels; combine with creamed corn, sliced red peppers, salt and pepper to taste. Pour into prepared casserole dish. Sprinkle bread crumbs on top.

3 Bake, uncovered, for 30 minutes. Serve hot.

roast asparagus with bacon

2 pounds asparagus, fresh
4 slices bacon
Salt and pepper, to taste

Serves 4 - 6

1 Preheat oven to 425°. Grease or spray a 9"x13" baking dish. Rinse asparagus and trim thick bottom edges (usually about 2 inches); dry on paper towels.

2 Fry bacon strips in large fry pan over medium-high heat. Remove when crisp; place on paper towels to drain. Crumble when cool, and set aside.

3 Add asparagus to bacon drippings and toss to coat; sauté for 1 - 2 minutes. (This may have to be done in several batches depending on size of fry pan.) Keeping all spears facing the same direction, transfer to prepared baking dish. Add crumbled bacon; sprinkle with salt and pepper, to taste.

4 Roast asparagus at 425° for approximately 15 minutes. Vegetables should be tender, yet slightly crisp. Serve hot.

Asparagus is one of the more elegant vegetables. This version is particularly tasty and will go with just about anything.

To make your last minute details less stressful, do Steps 1 - 3 in advance; cover and refrigerate. Roast when you are ready to serve.

baked barbequed beans

2 cans pork and beans **(16 ounces each)**
1/2 cup barbeque sauce
1/2 cup brown sugar
1 tablespoon mustard

4 slices bacon, uncooked

Serves 4 - 6

1 Preheat oven to 350°. Grease or spray a 2-quart baking dish.

2 Mix beans, barbeque sauce, brown sugar, and mustard. Transfer to baking dish.

3 Arrange bacon slices on top of beans.

4 Bake, uncovered, at 350° for 1 hour.

5 If desired, discard bacon. Serve with slotted spoon.

These wonderful sweet and spicy baked beans can also be prepared in advance through Step 3. Store, covered, in the refrigerator until one hour before serving.

This is the perfect accompaniment to hot dogs or hamburgers on the grill. I hope everyone at the party wants your recipe!

linguine with garlic butter

1/2 cup butter (1 stick)
1/4 cup olive oil
1 tablespoon dried parsley
1/2 teaspoon garlic powder
1/2 teaspoon salt

16 ounces linguine

Garnish: fresh parsley

Serves 4 - 6

1 Combine butter, olive oil, dried parsley, garlic powder and salt in saucepan. Cook over medium heat until butter is melted; stir as needed to blend all ingredients.

2 Cook linguine according to package directions, shortening cooking time suggested by a few minutes so that pasta is still slightly firm (al dente). Drain.

3 Toss butter mixture with hot, drained pasta; transfer to a serving dish. Sprinkle dried or snipped fresh parsley on top for garnish.

This is a perfect accompaniment to broiled chops, chicken or seafood. If you can't find linguine, use fettucine. Both are elegant.

While dried parsley is fine for the garnish, and certainly the easiest, a little snipped fresh parsley is inexpensive. Be sure to use clean kitchen shears.

classic mashed potatoes

2 pounds baking potatoes
1/4 cup butter **(1/2 stick)**
1/2 cup milk
1/2 cup sour cream
1 teaspoon salt
1/2 teaspoon white pepper

Serves 4

Everyone likes mashed potatoes... and they seem to go with almost anything.

Here is the simplest and best recipe I have tried. The trick is to mash while the potatoes are still very hot.

While the potatoes are boiling, tidy up the kitchen or set the table.

1 Peel potatoes completely; rinse well with cold water. Slice into pieces about 1 inch wide. Place in large pot; add enough water to cover potatoes. Bring to a boil.

2 Continue to boil, uncovered, until potatoes are soft, about 25 minutes. Drain; return drained potatoes to same pot.

3 While potatoes are hot, mash in butter. Then add milk, sour cream, salt and white pepper. Mash and mix with potato masher until all ingredients are well blended. For a creamier texture, add a little more milk, sour cream or butter. Transfer to serving bowl; serve hot.

The vegetable peeler and potato masher... two invaluable tools to have in your kitchen. If you don't have them, go immediately to the store and buy them!

With these simple gadgets and a little milk and butter, you can easily make the most perfect mashed potatoes. Hot creamy mashed potatoes are a comfort food... especially with an extra pat of butter on top.

smashed red potatoes with garlic

2 pounds red potatoes
1/4 cup butter (1/2 stick)
1 cup milk
1/2 teaspoon garlic powder
1/2 teaspoon salt
1/2 teaspoon black pepper

Serves 4

This recipe is very similar to the previous one for Classic Mashed Potatoes because these basic ingredients are the easiest and best! Be sure to add butter and milk while potatoes are still very hot.

I really can't tell you how much garlic powder, salt and pepper to use... you'll just have to taste-test. It's best to start with a small amount and then add accordingly.

1 Scrub potatoes under running water; then partially peel. With tip of potato peeler remove any blemished areas. Cut into chunks approximately 1 inch wide.

2 Place in large pot; add enough water to cover potatoes. Bring to a boil. Continue to boil, uncovered, until potatoes are soft, about 20 minutes. Drain; return drained potatoes to same pot.

3 While potatoes are hot, mash in butter. Then add milk, garlic powder, salt and black pepper. Mash with potato masher until ingredients are well blended and all milk has been absorbed. Appearance should seem chunky, rather than creamy, with potato skins visible. Transfer to serving bowl; serve hot.

roast potatoes

2 pounds potatoes
1/2 cup vegetable oil
Garlic salt and black pepper

Serves 4 - 6

Making this is like playing with your food - before you eat it. Be sure to start with clean hands.

Use any type of potatoes that you like. However, Idaho baking potatoes are the easiest to handle. All amounts given are only approximate.

A metal spatula is handy to remove potatoes from baking dish when serving.

1 Preheat oven to 425°.

2 Scrub potatoes under running water; then peel. With tip of potato peeler remove any blackened areas. Cut potatoes into chunks about 1 - 2 inches wide.

3 In large bowl, using hands, combine potatoes with oil. Coat all sides well.

4 Transfer to oblong baking dish. Season liberally with garlic salt and pepper. Roast uncovered for 45 minutes at 425°. Potatoes should be browned and crispy on outside, soft and moist on inside.

5 Serve immediately. Have salt and pepper available on the table.

Have fun with these potatoes! As you coat the potatoes with oil, actually *feel* them. Do not measure anything (I gave you an amount of 1/2 cup to have available, but you might not need that much). You will know when the amounts are right. Same with seasonings - sprinkle the garlic salt and pepper until it looks right. To repeat, there is no right or wrong! When you learn to cook this way, it's faster, easier and more like play than work. You won't believe how creative you are.

When baking cookies or cakes (or anything with leavening) it's usually important to measure the ingredients. But, when cooking, measurements are less important than personal taste preferences.

If you prefer the potatoes a little crispier, bake a few minutes longer. You want softer on the outside? ... bake a few minutes less. You get the idea..... They can stay warm in a low oven (250°) for a long time.

roast sweet potatoes

2 pounds sweet potatoes
1/2 cup vegetable oil
Garlic salt and black pepper

Serves 4 - 6

If this sounds similar to the Roast Potatoes two pages earlier, it is. But the flavor is so completely different with sweet potatoes (often called yams), Roast Sweet Potatoes deserves its own page. Also, you will note that the presentation is different, since the potatoes are sliced into thin rounds rather than chunks.

1 Preheat oven to 425°.

2 Scrub potatoes under running water; then peel. Remove any blackened areas. Cut potatoes into round slices approximately 1/2 inch thick.

3 In large bowl, using hands, combine potatoes with oil. Coat all sides well.

4 Layer slices in oblong baking dish in an overlapping pattern (envision a stack of round crackers laid on its side). Season liberally with garlic salt and pepper. Roast uncovered for 45 minutes at 425°. Potatoes should be browned and crispy on outside, soft and moist on inside.

5 Serve immediately. Have salt and pepper available on the table.

rice with sweet peas

2 cups quick-cooking white rice
1 cup sweet peas, frozen
2 cups water
1 tablespoon olive oil
1/2 teaspoon salt

Optional garnish:
1/4 cup Parmesan cheese, grated

Serves 4 - 6

Easy and colorful, this is a good accompaniment for almost any broiled seafood or pork entrée.

Save the remainder of the frozen peas for a later use. They are always good tossed in a salad.

1 Combine rice, frozen peas, water, oil and salt in saucepan. Stir well to mix. Using high heat, bring to a boil.

2 As soon as water starts to rapidly boil, remove from heat and cover. Let stand for 5 minutes, still covered.

3 Stir with fork to fluff; garnish with Parmesan cheese, if desired. Serve hot.

grown-up macaroni and cheese

16 ounces shell macaroni
2 tablespoons butter
1 cup light cream
16 ounces Velveeta ® cheese product
1/2 cup Parmesan cheese, grated
Salt and white pepper

Note: Can substitute milk for the light cream if less richness is desired.

Serves 6 - 8

When Grown-up Macaroni and Cheese is served with a platter of hot dogs, a simple meal becomes elegant. Buy cookies for dessert.

For a unique serving presentation, pour entire mixture into greased casserole dish and broil for several minutes until top is slightly browned and crispy. Watch carefully to prevent burning.

1 Bring 4 quarts water to a boil in a large saucepan. Add sprinkle of salt and all of macaroni, stirring well. Continue to boil, uncovered, for 7 - 9 minutes until pasta is soft, but still firm.

2 Remove shells to drainer in sink, and dispose of all boiling water.

3 Using same pot, heat butter, cream and Velveeta® cheese, cut into chunks. Continue to cook slowly, stirring often, until all cheese is melted. When mixture is smooth, add grated Parmesan cheese and salt and white pepper to taste.

4 Return macaroni to pot and stir well. Serve hot.

If you can't wash the pot right after cooking, fill with hot soapy water and let it sit in the sink. This will prevent cooked-on cheese from becoming too hard to clean when your guests have gone home.

honey glazed carrots with ginger

1 package frozen carrots (16 ounces)
1/4 cup butter (1/2 stick)
1/4 cup honey
1 teaspoon ground ginger

Serves 4

1 Using 2-quart saucepan, boil carrots in small amount of water until crisp tender, about 5 minutes. Remove carrots to drainer in sink, disposing of all cooking liquid.

2 Using same saucepan, melt butter. Stir in honey and ground ginger. Add carrots; mix well to coat.

3 Transfer to serving bowl; serve hot.

Note: This can be kept warm in a low oven up to one hour if necessary.

These glazed carrots are a colorful accompaniment to any grilled meat or poultry. The ginger adds a nice perk.

They can be made in advance and reheated in the oven, if you like.

pineapple with cheese

1 can crushed pineapple (20 ounces)
2 cups shredded Cheddar cheese (8 ounces)
1/2 cup baking mix (such as Bisquick®)
1/2 cup sugar

Serves 6

1 Preheat oven to 350°. Grease or spray 2-quart baking dish.

2 Combine shredded cheese with baking mix and sugar. Mix in crushed pineapple, including juice.

3 Pour into greased baking dish.

4 Bake, uncovered, at 350° for 45 minutes. Let cool for 5 minutes before serving.

This is a terrific side dish for pork chops or baked ham. Its mellow sweetness offsets a spicy or well seasoned main entrée.

You can buy Cheddar cheese in the dairy department already shredded; or use your food processor to easily shred fresh cheese yourself.

mandarin marshmallow mix

1 can mandarin oranges (11 ounces)
1 can pineapple chunks (20 ounces)
1 cup miniature marshmallows
1 cup coconut, flaked
1 cup sour cream

Serves 4 - 6

Mandarin Marshmallow Mix is a sweet and creamy accompaniment instead of the usual green salad.

While this can be served immediately, the flavors are even better if prepared one day in advance and kept chilled in the refrigerator, tightly covered, until ready to serve.

1 Drain cans of mandarin oranges and pineapple chunks. Combine fruit with marshmallows and coconut.

2 Add sour cream; continue to mix until all ingredients are well blended.

3 Cover with plastic wrap; chill until ready to serve.

orange cream

2 packages orange gelatin (3 ounces each)
2 cups boiling water
2 cups vanilla ice cream, softened

Optional: 1/2 cup chopped pecans

Serves 6 - 8

1 Using large mixing bowl, dissolve gelatin in boiling water. Add ice cream and mix well.

2 Use cooking spray to lightly grease gelatin mold (1-quart or larger). Pour mixture into mold and refrigerate, covered, until set. Allow 6 hours.

3 If you are adding optional chopped pecans, mix them in gently after gelatin has chilled for about 30 minutes, but has not yet fully set.

4.To unmold gelatin, dip mold into bowl of hot water for a few seconds. Loosen edges with knife and invert onto serving platter.

Experiment with different flavors of gelatin. To accompany a pork dinner, try raspberry. With lamb, you might try lime. Orange or lemon flavors seem to go well with poultry, although cherry would be nice for a holiday dinner.

This can be made at least one day in advance and kept in the refrigerator, covered.

desserts

This Guide will not include a recipe for homemade apple pie! Apple pie is simply too easy to buy - either fresh or frozen. Both can be inexpensive and excellent. If you want to bake such a dessert to make your home smell wonderful, select one of the many frozen varieties and pop it into the oven as the package directs. Your guests simply don't care "who made the pie". And you must always remember, I don't want you to be too worn out to enjoy your guests! However, this Guide does suggest serving the apple pie with rich vanilla ice cream - definitely purchased ready-made.

For different ideas, experiment with a few of the easy and well-liked recipes on the following pages. Also, be sure to see the chapters "Chocolate is a Necessary Food Group" and "Holidays" for more favorites.

easy peanut butter cookies

1 cup peanut butter
(smooth or chunky)
1 cup sugar
1 egg

Parchment paper

Makes 12 large cookies

This is the easiest home-baked cookie recipe I could find. If you want a smoother texture, use an electric mixer instead of a fork to combine ingredients.

Parchment paper is great to have on hand for baking. It eliminates the need to grease the pan, and clean-up is faster and easier.

1 Preheat oven to 375°. Cut parchment paper to fit baking sheet.

2 Using a large mixing bowl, beat egg with a fork. Mix in sugar, then peanut butter, until all ingredients are well blended.

3 Roll dough into small balls; flatten slightly. Place on prepared baking sheet.

4 Bake for 15 minutes at 375°. Cookies will appear soft, but will become more firm when cooled.

lemonade pie

9” graham cracker pie crust

1 can lemonade concentrate (6 ounces)
1 can sweetened condensed milk (14 ounces)
1 container whipped topping (8 ounces)

Optional: lemon slices for garnish

Serves 8

This sweet and tart dessert is perfect for beginning cooks. So easy, so pretty, so good.

For variety, try frozen limeade or frozen daiquiri mix instead of lemonade.

1 Thaw lemonade; combine with sweetened condensed milk in a large mixing bowl. Using a spatula to scrape sides and bottom of the bowl, thoroughly mix in whipped topping. All ingredients should be completely blended.

2 Spoon mixture into pie crust; cover with plastic wrap. Chill until firm, about 6 hours.

3 When ready to serve, garnish with thin slices of lemon.

cherry cheesecake

9" graham cracker pie crust

1 package cream cheese **(8 ounces)**
2 eggs
1/2 cup sugar
1 tablespoon lemon juice
1 teaspoon vanilla

1 can cherry pie filling **(21 ounces)**

Serves 8

1 Preheat oven to 325°. Soften cream cheese in microwave for 20 seconds.

2 With electric mixer, beat eggs until frothy. Add softened cream cheese, sugar, lemon juice and vanilla; continue to mix on medium speed for about one minute.

3 Spoon cream cheese mixture into graham cracker pie crust. Bake at 325° for 40 minutes. Remove from oven and cool.

4 To serve: Slice pie and place on individual plates; spoon pie filling on top.

This cheesecake has been a favorite for generations. Sweet, smooth and creamy, it is enjoyed by all.

If you don't like cherries, use any pie filling that you do like. When strawberries are in season, mix sliced or whole fruit with a little sugar for a fabulous topping. See the Strawberry Shortcake recipes for further directions.

blueberry cobbler

1 stick butter, melted (1/2 cup)
1 cup self-rising flour
1 cup sugar
1 cup milk

1 can blueberry pie filling (21 ounces)

Optional: whipped topping or vanilla ice cream, for serving

Serves 10 - 12

This is a terrific dessert to make for a large group. Don't like blueberries? This is equally good with any pie filling of your choice. Cherry cobbler is my second favorite.

It is very important to use self-rising flour - not regular flour. Self-rising flour contains the necessary leavening ingredients.

1 Preheat oven to 400°. While oven is heating, melt butter in a 9"x13" baking dish.

2 Add self-rising flour, sugar and milk to melted butter; combine all together with fork. Batter will be slightly lumpy.

3 Spoon pie filling on top of batter. Do not mix! Bake at 400° for 30 minutes. Serve hot.

fresh fruit
with sour cream topping

Fresh fruit in season...

there's nothing better to end your meal. Rinse the fruit well, dry on paper towels and arrange on a pretty platter or large plate. Provide the bowl of topping on the side for guests to help themselves.

Serve with simple sugar cookies or shortbread, if you like.

Fruit possibilities:

Raspberries, blueberries, strawberries, pineapple chunks, grape clusters, melon cubes, sliced apples and bananas

The topping:

Mix together well -

1 cup sour cream
1/4 cup honey
1 tablespoon lemon juice

fast and easy strawberry shortcake

Strawberries, frozen (16 ounces)
Pound cake, fresh or frozen
Whipped topping (8 ounces)

Serves 8

Note: If possible buy a package of frozen strawberries with heavy syrup. If fruit does not include syrup, mix in 1/4 cup sugar while fruit is thawing.

1 Thaw frozen berries.

2 If cake is frozen, thaw according to package directions. With sharp knife, cut into 8 slices.

3 Spoon whipped topping onto cake slices.

4 Top with berrries.

For strawberry lovers who don't have much time, this dessert is the one to choose!

With all parts of the recipe pre-purchased, you just need to slice, spoon and you are ready to go. The only thing you will need to mix is the strawberries with a little sugar if you buy the sliced or whole frozen berries without syrup.

Unless... you buy the cake, buy the whipped topping and use fresh berries, utilizing Step 3 of the following recipe of Deluxe Strawberry Shortcake on the next page!!!!

deluxe strawberry shortcake

I know this seems complicated, and most of you will skip it for the time being, but when you really want something spectacular this is it.

Some day when you have nothing else to do but play in the kitchen, get together these ingredients and try it. It is a good choice when all other parts of the meal are either purchased or brought in by guests. How about a party with no dinner - just dessert?

Note: Strawberries can be rinsed and sliced in advance, but not mixed with sugar until one hour before serving; shortcake can be made in advance and covered tightly (not refrigerated); and whipped cream can be made in advance, covered tightly and kept refrigerated.

Shortcake:
2 cups baking mix (such as Bisquick®)
1/2 teaspoon salt
1/4 cup sugar
1/4 cup butter (1/2 stick)**, softened**
3/4 cup half and half
Parchment paper for baking

Fruit filling:
1 quart strawberries
1/2 cup sugar

Whipped cream:
2 cups heavy cream, chilled
3 tablespoons sugar

Serves 8

1 Preheat oven to 425°. Cut parchment paper to fit baking sheet.

2 Chill mixing bowl and beaters well for best results in whipping cream. (Use freezer if you only have a few minutes.)

3 Wash strawberries under cool water; remove hulls with tip of sharp knife, then slice. In a large bowl, mix sliced strawberries with 1/2 cup sugar; set aside.

4 To prepare shortcake, combine baking mix, salt and 1/4 cup sugar in large bowl. Cut butter into 8 chunks and add to mix. Using up-and-down wrist motion with pastry cutter, stir all together just until butter pieces are slightly smaller than pea-size. Do not overwork... ingredients should not be smooth at this point. Add half-and-half and stir with fork just until liquid is absorbed. If you are unsure, under-mixing is better than over-mixing for tender biscuits.

5 Using tablespoon, drop onto parchment-covered baking sheet, making 8 uneven, lumpy mounds! If dough is very sticky, you might need to assist with fingers. Bake for 12 - 14 minutes in 425° oven, until tops are slightly browned and shortbread feels barely firm (not mushy) to your touch. Set aside to cool.

A pastry cutter is an inexpensive, hand-held gadget easily purchased at all stores featuring kitchenware.

It is sometimes referred to as a pastry blender. It blends dry ingredients in a perfect way.

6 To prepare whipped cream, add chilled heavy cream to chilled small mixing bowl. Setting speed on high, mix continually for several minutes until soft peaks form. Sprinkle in sugar (up to 3 tablespoons) as desired for sweetness.

7 You are ready to serve! With sharp knife, slice cooled shortbreads in half. Spoon whipped cream and strawberries alternately onto bottom half of shortbread, then replace top half to finish.

pears with wine sauce

1 large can pear halves (29 ounces)
1/2 cup red wine
2 tablespoons butter
2 tablespoons brown sugar

1 quart vanilla ice cream

Serves 4

This recipe is good to consider because other than the pears you should already have most of the ingredients.

Use an inexpensive red wine. Or... substitute brandy if you prefer.

1 Drain pears and combine with wine in non-metal bowl. Cover and let pears marinate in refrigerator for two hours.

2 When ready to serve, preheat oven to 450°. While oven is heating, melt the butter in small baking dish. Spoon pears, including a little of the wine, on top of the butter. With fingers, sprinkle brown sugar on top of pears.

3 Bake for about 5 minutes, or until fruit is very hot. Check occasionally to be sure the sugar is not burning.

4 Serve immediately with a scoop of vanilla ice cream on the side.

Invite a few friends over after the movies just for dessert...

make the dessert in advance,
have the coffee pot ready and the table set.

Or... be more casual and place everything out buffet style to allow guests to help themselves.

three **ingredients** or less

This could be the most useful chapter in the book for brides and grooms inexperienced in the kitchen. And, even as you gain in your expertise, these recipes can be enjoyed for many years. They are simple and oh-so-delicious!

I have given you amounts to be used for most ingredients, but these are certainly not absolute. Like this book, the amounts listed are simply a guide, and may be readily increased or decreased depending on your personal preference.

You might note that I have only included Appetizers and Entrées in this chapter. Too many sub-categories for each part of the meal is too confusing for even the author! The "Three Ingredients or Less" Drinks, Soups, Salads, Accompaniments and Desserts are definitely in the book but are incorporated under those headings in The Main Event chapter.

For those of you counting, the "three ingredients or less" does not include the seasonings.

Experiment... enjoy... have fun!

three ingredients or less...
appetizers

sweet and salty mix

1 cup M&M's® chocolate candies
1 cup salted peanuts
1 cup raisins

Serves 4 - 6

1 Mix.

2 Serve.

I don't know if there is a real name for this, but I do know this mix is very popular.

This salty and sweet combination is a delicious munchie to accompany drinks.

salsa with cream cheese

8 ounces cream cheese
1 cup chunky salsa

Tortilla chips for serving

Serves 4 - 6

1 Soften cream cheese slightly; drain excess liquid from salsa.

2 Using fork, mix cream cheese with salsa - just barely - so that cream cheese is still in chunks. Over-mixing will make it goopy.

You might want to double these ingredients if you have a large or particularly ravenous crowd.

Salsa and cream cheese are two ingredients to always have in the refrigerator for unexpected guests.

marinated peppers and cheese

8 ounces cream cheese
1 cup marinated hot pepper mix
(also known as Giardeniera)

Cut up veggies for serving

Serves 4 - 6

1 Drain peppers.

2 Using food processor fitted with metal mixing blade, combine cream cheese and peppers for about 20 seconds. Mixture should be smooth with bits of peppers still visible.

3 Garnish with whole pepper, if available.

This is a creamy, yet hearty dip with just the right amount of spice.

Baby carrots, sliced cucumbers and celery sticks would be good veggies to accompany Marinated Peppers and Cheese.

The hot pepper mix known as Giardeniera can be found in the pickles department of your grocer.

bacon crisps

10 slices bacon, uncooked and cut into thirds

1 can pineapple chunks
1 can whole water chestnuts

Wooden toothpicks

Makes 30 appetizers

Pineapple chunks and water chestnuts are only two of a great many possibilities. Fresh melon in season would be delicious, as would mini-meatballs (thawed first).

For a very elegant presentation, try sea scallops or baby shrimp seasoned with a little garlic salt and pepper. Anything that can be secured with a toothpick and not melt will work.

1 Wrap a pineapple chunk with small piece of bacon and secure both ends with a plain wooden toothpick. Do the same with a water chestnut. (If items being wrapped are too large, slice in half.) Repeat until all bacon is used.

2 Place in single layer in an ungreased pan. Broil for approximately 7 - 10 minutes, or until bacon is crispy. Turn pieces over to brown underside. (Keep the oven door slightly open to allow heat to circulate; watch bacon to prevent burning.)

3 Arrange on serving platter and serve hot.

hot artichoke dip

1 can artichoke hearts (14 ounces)
drained and cut-up

1 cup grated Parmesan cheese
1 cup mayonaise
Garlic powder

Serves 6 - 8

When I was a young bride almost 30 years ago, this dip was served at almost every party because it was so very good. It is still that good.

To vary the taste, you might want to try substituting grated Romano for the Parmesan cheese. If you want a smoother dip, mix all ingredients in a blender or food processor for about 30 seconds before baking.

1 With fork or potato masher, break apart the artichoke hearts. Mix together with grated cheese and mayonaise. Add a pinch of garlic powder, to taste.

2 Spoon into a greased casserole dish; bake uncovered at 350° for 30 minutes. Serve hot with your favorite crackers.

three ingredients or less...
entrées

I am beginning this section with chicken recipes... lots of chicken recipes... since poultry is well-liked by almost everyone. And, compared to most varieties of beef, pork or seafood, it is relatively inexpensive as a main course.

One note about chicken, however - white meat (the breast portion) tends to cook more quickly than dark meat (the leg portion). Also, boneless chicken needs only about one-half the time as bone-in chicken.

So... if you are cooking all white meat, shorten the cooking time by about 10 or 15 minutes per recipe. The cooking times listed are given with dark meat in mind to make sure that none of the chicken would be undercooked. Much better a little overcooked than undercooked! Regarding boneless versus bone-in, if you differ from the recipe as given (and please do if you like!), just remember to adjust cooking time accordingly. As an example, chicken breasts with bone in usually require about 45-50 minutes of cooking, whereas boneless chicken breasts only need about 25-30 minutes to be fully done.

Have I confused you yet? It will become clear only after you start.

garlicky chicken

8 pieces chicken, bone-in, with skin
1/2 cup butter (1 stick)
2 teaspoons garlic powder
Salt and pepper

Optional garnish: lemon slices

Serves 4 - 6

1 Preheat oven to 375°. Spray or grease large baking dish.

2 Rinse chicken in cool water; dry with paper towels. Arrange in baking dish, single layer, skin side up. Sprinkle well with salt and pepper.

3 In large glass measuring cup, melt butter in microwave (about 45 seconds). Add garlic and stir. Brush or spoon evenly onto chicken.

4 Bake uncovered for approximately one hour.

5 Transfer chicken to platter; spoon pan juices over chicken. Garnish with lemon slices, if desired. Serve immediately.

This is very garlicky! You might choose to use less powder.

A good accompaniment to this dish would be wild rice. Buy a package of the quick-cooking variety.

A simple green salad and rolls complete the dinner.

All ovens have their own distinct personalities... some are "hotter" than others. After some use, you will get to know your own oven's temperature gauge. The degrees of heat... and lengths of cooking time... given in these recipes are guides, but might need to be adjusted if you find your foods are either cooking too fast or too slow in relation to the instructions as written.

I tell you this not to complicate matters, but rather to explain if your meal is ready sooner or later than expected.

orange raspberry chicken

8 pieces chicken, bone-in, with skin
1 can mandarin oranges (11 ounces)
1 cup raspberry preserves
Salt and pepper

Serves 4 - 6

1 Preheat oven to 375°. Spray or grease large baking dish.

2 Rinse chicken in cool water; dry with paper towels. Arrange in baking dish, single layer, skin side up. Sprinkle well with salt and pepper. Drain mandarin oranges; place around chicken.

3 Using a non-metal bowl or measuring glass, melt raspberry preserves in microwave (about 1 minute). Pour over chicken.

4 Bake uncovered for approximately one hour. (Check after 45 minutes: if chicken is browning too quickly, reduce heat and cover loosely with foil for the last 15 minutes.)

5 Transfer chicken to platter; spoon pan juices over chicken. Serve immediately.

Rice is a good choice to accompany this flavorful chicken. If using non-instant rice, begin cooking immediately after chicken is in the oven for synchronized timing.

sherry chicken

8 pieces chicken, bone-in, with skin
1/4 cup butter (1/2 stick)
1 cup sherry wine
Garlic salt and pepper
Paprika

Serves 4 - 6

1 Preheat oven to 350°. While oven is heating, melt butter in 9"x13" baking dish; when melted, pour in sherry.

2 Rinse chicken in cool water; dry with paper towels. Dip pieces into butter and sherry; coating well on all sides. Arrange chicken in baking dish, skin side up, single layer.

3 Sprinkle with garlic salt, pepper and paprika. Cover with foil.

4 Bake, covered, for 30 minutes. Uncover; continue to bake for additional 30 minutes.

5 Remove chicken to platter; spoon pan juices over chicken. Serve immediately.

Thin egg noodles cooked according to package directions would be a good choice to serve with this crisp and golden chicken.

Use your gravy boat to offer your guests the excellent pan juices.

beef brisket in beer

3 - 4 pounds beef brisket
1 package dry onion soup (1 ounce)
1 can beer (12 ounces)

Serves 6 - 8

Five hours is a long time, but the oven heat is low. This combination makes the brisket very tender. Your parents and grandparents will love it and think you are so talented!

If entertaining your friends, slice the beef and add your favorite barbeque sauce. Serve on buns with cole slaw, pickles and chips.

1 Preheat oven to 275°. Rinse brisket under cool water; place in large baking pan.

2 With hands, sprinkle dry onion soup on both sides of beef; rub in, coating as well as possible. Pour beer over beef. Before cooking, make sure fat side of brisket is on top.

3 Tightly cover pan with foil. Bake for 5 hours.

4 When cooking is complete, remove foil very carefully to allow steam to escape.

5 If serving immediately, allow to cool slightly. With very sharp knife, remove excess fat; slice against the grain. Arrange on serving platter. Pan juices will make delicious gravy. If "au jus" is preferred, simply pour liquid through strainer. Serve hot.

A wooden cutting board and an electric knife are a good combination to use when slicing your brisket. The first few cuts should be to remove the top layer of fat; then all beef served will be leaner. Have a serving plate nearby and transfer portions as cut.

All beef slices more uniformly when cooled slightly. And, remember, always cut against the grain for maximum tenderness.

When re-heating, place slices in pan juices, covered, with a low oven (300° or less).

barbequed ribs

4 pounds spareribs
1 cup barbeque sauce

Serves 6

It doesn't get any easier than this! To facilitate easier cleanup of roasting pan, line with heavy aluminum foil prior to cooking.

Serve with garlic bread, tossed salad, pickles and chips. Don't forget... lots of napkins.

1 Preheat oven to 300°. Wipe ribs with paper towels; place in large roasting pan.

2 Pour barbeque sauce on top of ribs. Cover pan with aluminum foil.

3 Cook for 3 hours at 300°. Remove foil covering; baste with pan juices. Continue to roast, uncovered, for an additional 30 minutes.

4 Transfer to a large platter and serve.

Note: Ribs can be prepared in advance and reheated for 30 minutes, covered, at 300°.

marinated flank steak

2 pounds flank steak
(sometimes called "skirt" steak)

1/3 cup honey
1/3 cup soy sauce

Serves 4 - 6

Marinade for Flank Steak can be started up to 24 hours in advance.

Have your electric knife and cutting board ready for last minute slicing.

Smashed Red Potatoes with Garlic is a perfect accompaniment.

1 At least 4 hours prior to meal, prepare marinade by mixing honey with soy sauce in shallow dish.

2 With fork, pierce steak well on both sides. Place steak in marinade, coating both sides. Cover; refrigerate until ready to cook.

3 Immediately before dinner, preheat broiler. Spoon marinade over beef.

4 With broiler pan on center rack of oven, broil for about 5 minutes; turn steak over, baste with more marinade; broil approximately 5 additional minutes. Check degree of rareness for individual preference.

5 Remove to cutting board; slice diagonally against the grain. Serve with pan juices which have been thoroughly cooked.

Honey, brown sugar, soy sauce and beer!

You are probably noticing I am suggesting the same ingredients again and again. The honey and brown sugar are easy sweeteners, the soy sauce adds garlic and spice, while the beer (wine, bourbon, etc.) tenderizes and adds flavor at the same time. Please substitute one sweetener for another, or wine instead of beer. If you desire a non-alcoholic liquid for the marinade, use your favorite carbonated cola... although diet versions do not work as well. You will soon develop your own favorites.

Remember: experiment... enjoy... have fun! There are no mistakes, just variations.

salmon with brown sugar glaze

4 salmon steaks
1/3 cup brown sugar
1/2 cup soy sauce

Serves 4

1 Preheat oven to 400°. Grease or spray baking dish.

2 Press brown sugar onto both sides of all salmon steaks; place in baking dish, single layer. Pour soy sauce on top.

3 Bake for approximately 10 minutes, uncovered. If salmon steaks are very thick, increase cooking time to 12 - 15 minutes. No need to turn salmon over.

4 Cooking is complete when salmon is flaky and no longer translucent. Serve pan juices in gravy boat or small bowl.

This might be the most delicious salmon you have ever tasted. It's a great change from the usual beef or chicken dinner.

Serve with Roast Asparagus with Bacon or Classic Mashed Potatoes, hot buttered rolls and your favorite wine.

what a crock

The slow cooker is an appliance which should be in all newlyweds' kitchens. Its merits are invaluable, most especially when entertaining. Recipe preparation is generally minimal and once the cooker is turned on, your work is usually complete. With some of the newer models, timers allow for the unit to either turn on or off automatically so you can be away for long periods and still have a perfect dinner. When cooking is finished the "Keep Warm" setting is automatically activated.

The recipes included here have been selected for extra ease. So... pick a recipe, assemble the ingredients, fill up the pot and take a nap.

sweet and spicy meatballs

Prepared meatballs, frozen (24 - 32 ounces)
1 jar grape jelly (18 ounces)
1 bottle chili sauce (12 ounces)

Serves 8 for appetizers

Note: Amount of meatballs does not need to be exact. Bag sizes vary; use whatever amount you like, just making sure there is enough sauce to cover all balls.

My son Eric could eat these meatballs three times a day, every day. Have plenty of toothpicks on hand for guests to serve themselves.

1 Mix jelly and chili sauce directly in slow cooker; add frozen meatballs and stir, making sure all meatballs are coated well. No need to defrost.

2 Cook on High power, covered, for 2 hours.

3 Transfer to serving bowl. Have available a serving spoon and small plates, with toothpicks nearby.

rio grandé cheese dip

2 pounds Velveeta® cheese (32 ounces)
1 can diced tomatoes with green chilies (10 ounces)

Serves 10 - 12 for appetizers

Note: For more spice (but less dip), use only 16 ounces (1 pound) of cheese for each can of tomatoes with chilies. If dip becomes too thick, stir in 2 tablespoons of milk.

This is fabulous on a cold day when watching a football game. Serve with toast rounds or tortilla chips.

1 Cut cheese into chunks; place in bottom of slow cooker. Slightly drain tomatoes and add to cheese.

2 Cook on High power, covered, for 1 hour.

3 Stir and serve.

rio grandé tortillas

1 pound Velveeta® cheese (16 ounces)
1 can diced tomatoes with green chilies (10 ounces)

1-1/2 pounds ground beef
Salt and pepper

8 flour tortillas (soft)

Optional: chopped lettuce and tomatoes, for serving

Makes 8 servings

Yes... this is similar to the recipe for Rio Grandé Cheese Dip on the preceding page. With added ground beef and tortillas, you have the main entrée for a quick and easy meal. My friend Jay tells me it's one of his favorites.

Serve with green salad and beer.

1 Cut cheese into chunks; place in bottom of slow cooker. Slightly drain tomatoes and add to cheese.

2 Cook on High power, covered, for 1 hour.

3 While cheese sauce is cooking, crumble ground beef in non-stick fry pan. Sprinkle with salt and pepper. Cook over medium heat, uncovered, until meat begins to brown. Turn with spatula as needed to brown all meat evenly.

4 When ready to serve, wrap tortillas in foil and heat in hot oven (400°) for a few minutes until warmed and soft. Spoon cooked meat onto individual tortillas; cover with cheese sauce. Fold over sides envelope style to enclose meat and cheese; roll as best as possible. Serve hot.

brats and kraut

1 pound smoked bratwurst, fully cooked
1 large can sauerkraut (28 ounces)
2 tablespoons mustard
2 tablespoons brown sugar
1 teaspoon caraway seeds

Hot dog buns

Serves 4

1 Put all of sauerkraut, including liquid, into slow cooker. Mix in mustard, brown sugar and caraway seeds. Slice each brat in half lengthwise and place on top of kraut.

2 Replace cover; cook on High power for 2 hours.

3 Optional: Transfer to baking dish with brats on top; place under broiler momentarily to crisp and brown brats. Serve hot.

For more than four people (or very hungry guests), simply double amounts of ingredients. If you can't find fully cooked bratwurst, cook brats according to package directions before putting in slow cooker to remove extra fat.

Serve with potato salad from the deli and hot corn on the cob.

barbequed beef sandwiches

2 -3 pounds chuck roast
2 tablespoons vegetable oil
2 bottles barbeque sauce
1/2 cup beer
Salt and pepper

Hamburger buns
Pickles

Serves 4 - 6

Start this at least one night before your party. It can cook on Low heat all night while you sleep.

You need 2 bottles of barbeque sauce to have enough for cooking and extra for serving. Pass the pickles!

1 Wipe roast with damp paper towel. Sprinkle both sides with salt and pepper.

2 Using medium temperature, heat oil in large fry pan. Add meat and brown on all sides; about 2 minutes.

3 Pour 1/2-cup barbeque sauce (saving remainder of bottle for later) and 1/2-cup beer into slow cooker. Mix together with fork. Put in browned meat. Replace cover on slow cooker.

4 Cook on Low power for 8 hours.

5 When beef is fully cooked, but still hot, remove to large mixing bowl and break into chunks; then, using two forks, pull apart. It will look shredded.

6. Combine meat with two cups of bottled barbeque sauce and up to one cup of liquid from pot; continue to mix with fork. (There should be plenty of sauce so that meat can continue to absorb liquid as it cools.) Cover and refrigerate.

7 When ready to serve, reheat in covered saucepan over low heat on stovetop; or, transfer to casserole dish and heat in oven, covered, for 30 minutes at 300°. (If beef has absorbed all liquid and appears dry, add more barbeque sauce before heating.)

Serve with hash brown potatoes, frozen, prepared according to package directions, and baked beans.

Cooking this in advance gives you extra time to get your kitchen cleaned up well in advance of the party.

braised beef with vegetables and wine

2 -3 pounds beef brisket
2 tablespoons vegetable oil
Salt and pepper

1 cup red wine
1 package dry onion soup
1 large bag baby carrots, frozen
1 small can whole mushrooms

Serves 4 - 6

1 Wipe brisket with damp paper towel. Sprinkle both sides with salt and pepper.

2 Using medium heat, warm oil in large fry pan. Add meat and brown on both sides (about 1 minute).

3 Mix wine and dry onion soup in slow cooker. Put in browned meat (fat side up). Arrange carrots and mushrooms (drained) on top of meat. Replace cover on slow cooker. Cook on Low power for 8 - 10 hours.

4 Transfer beef to cutting board; with sharp knife, slice brisket against grain. Arrange slices in serving dish with vegetables and gravy spooned on top.

Braised Beef with Vegetables and Wine is an almost complete meal which can cook all day while you work. If you like, brown the meat and place remainder of ingredients in the cook bowl the night before; cover and refrigerate.

This recipe is designed to be served to your grandparents. They will be very happy! Good accompaniment would be Wide Egg Noodles (cooked according to package directions).

mediterranean meatballs

Prepared meatballs, frozen (32 ounces)
2 cans whole tomatoes (15 ounces each)
1 bottle Spanish olives (5 - 7 ounces)
1 onion, chopped
1 cup red wine

Serves 6 - 8

This is a wonderful Sunday night dinner for your family. It's so easy and good, you'll want to serve it again and again.

Prepare white rice according to package directions. If you are short on time, use quick-cooking rice. Ask your Mom to bring the salad.

1 Place all ingredients in slow cooker, including liquid from tomatoes and olives. Mix to combine. Replace cover.

2 Cook on High power for 3 hours.

3 Transfer to serving bowl. Serve over rice.

cas'-sou-let n.

French; a casserole of beans slowly baked with various meats and poultry

Reference: Webster's New World Dictionary of American English, Third College Edition, Copyright © 1988 by Simon & Schuster, Inc. NY

cassoulet

8 ounces smoked sausage, fully cooked
8 ounces skinless, boneless chicken thighs
3 carrots
1 cup white wine
2 cans Great Northern beans (15 ounces each)
2 cans diced tomatoes (14.5 ounces each)
2 teaspoons chicken bouillon
2 teaspoons Italian seasoning, dried
1/2 teaspoon garlic powder
1/4 teaspoon ground red pepper

Optional: grated Parmesan cheese

Serves 6

1 Rinse chicken; drain on paper towels. Cut sausage and chicken into bite-size pieces. Wash, peel and thinly slice carrots. Place all of the above in slow cooker.

2 Add wine, and all of beans and tomatoes, including can liquids. Stir in bouillon, Italian seasoning, garlic powder and ground red pepper.

3 Replace cover on slow cooker; cook on High power for 4 hours or Low power for 8 hours.

4 If desired, pass a small bowl of grated Parmesan cheese at the table.

OK... I know this recipe has a lot of ingredients. But many of them are easily obtained just by opening cans and the seasonings are common ones that you should have in your pantry. If you do not want to use fresh carrots, substitute one small package of frozen or one can of sliced carrots, drained. Did you notice how few instructions there are?

Serve with hot crusty bread and a bottle of wine.

holidays

Your first holiday dinner as a married couple! What could be more special? With a little creativity and ingenuity your home will become warm with the spirit of the season. Holidays are actually not much different than any other dinner - just a little fancier, perhaps, with a few more candles and floral decorations. This is definitely the occasion to bring out every beautiful piece of china, crystal and silver you own. Don't be hesitant to use partial placesettings mixed in with other assorted tableware. It will be a chance for you to coordinate. (And also a chance for your family to see what gifts you might like for future occasions!) Do, however, try to group the same types of silverware and glassware at the same placesetting wherever possible. Put your grandmother's candlesticks in the middle of the table with tall new tapers. Pine boughs add a festive touch. If it's Christmas, tie the napkins with cheery red ribbons, sprinkle a few shiny ornaments among the candles, and your table will be most elegant!

All guests will offer to bring something. Your proper response is... "yes-s-s... Thank you very much."

As host and hostess, your main task (after cleaning your home, of course) is to organize. Who will bring what? Do not...I repeat... do not attempt to prepare all foods. You will be frazzled and exhausted, and most likely will not have much fun.

My suggestion would be for you to provide the main entrée, and possibly one or two simple accompaniments. Usually a turkey is a good choice for the entrée. If you follow my instructions (stay close to the recipe on this one), your bird will be tender, moist, look like it should be on a magazine cover, and above all, be very easy. Baked ham is another excellent choice for the main dish. Of course, recipes and instructions follow.

Let's start with the turkey...

... where do you buy it? ... what size?
... fresh or frozen? ... whole turkey or just the breast?

So many questions! I have answers!! First, you buy it at the grocery store where you buy your other food items. Many stores will have turkey specials preceding a holiday, so watch the papers for sales.

Second, the size you need to buy depends on the amount of guests you are having. It is better to over-estimate rather than under-estimate, since turkey leftovers are almost as delicious as the original dinner. But, generally, allow 3/4 pound uncooked weight of bone-in turkey per person.

"Fresh or frozen?" is a good question that causes even seasoned cooks to disagree on the answer. If you have time to thaw the turkey and space in your refrigerator to do so, there really is no difference in taste. There is, however, usually a big difference in the cost. If you buy a frozen turkey, you should allow up to four days for poultry to completely thaw in the refrigerator. (Thawing at room temperature can cause parts of the poultry to spoil.)

... and last, go for the whole bird rather than just the breast. Aside from the fact that many people prefer dark meat over white, the completed roast whole turkey, golden and crisp, just looks so very grand! If you insist that no one who will be at your table likes dark meat, buy a boneless turkey breast. The method of cooking will be the same.

What if ... it's the night before the holiday and the turkey is still frozen? Do not panic. Leave turkey in its original plastic wrap and place in a sink full of cold water. (You might need to add ice to keep the water cold.) Thawing with this method should take up to 8 hours for large turkeys, but less time, of course, if the bird is already partially thawed. Do NOT cook the turkey if it is still frozen at all! It will cook improperly and could even cause food poisoning.

Do not remove any of the plastic wrap until completely thawed and ready to cook.

step-by-step instructions

If you can read these instructions, you can make a perfect turkey. There are several ways to do it, but I'm going to give you failproof directions using a disposable oven bag. If you follow step-by-step (after you have read these past few pages), I promise your results will be spectacular with very little effort.

Turkey and seasonings you will need...

Turkey
Vegetable oil
Flour
Poultry seasoning
Salt and pepper

Optional: stuffing

Supplies you will need...

Large roasting pan

(If using a disposable foil pan, which is recommended for easy cleanup, place it on top of the heavy bottom part of your oven broiler pan for additional support when lifting the turkey in and out of the oven.)

2 heavy-duty oven mitts

Meat thermometer (unless your bird already has a pop-up timer)

Clear disposable oven bag, turkey size, 19"x23"

Arrange oven racks so that turkey will be centered in the oven. Try using the second rack from bottom, removing top racks if necessary.

If you live in an area where you cannot get an oven cooking bag, you can still have a perfect turkey. Preparation directions are basically the same, but cooking time is longer. Refer to the instructions included with your turkey.

roast turkey

Whole turkey, thawed
Vegetable oil
Poultry seasoning
Salt and pepper

Oven bag, turkey size (approximately 19"x23")
2 tablespoons flour

Varied servings, depending on size of turkey (see preceding pages)

Preparing a turkey with an oven roasting bag is the easiest and most failproof way to produce glorious results.

When you use the clear roasting bag, there is no basting, very little clean-up, and you do not have to continually "check". The poultry skin will turn a crisp and golden brown with no fear of burning.

Whether or not to "stuff" the turkey is your choice.

1 Preheat oven to 350°. Measure 2 tablespoons flour into the oven roasting bag, and shake to completely coat inside of bag.

2 Cut away all wrapping from turkey. Remove giblets and all miscellaneous pieces from both cavities (carefully check inside front and back). These parts can be saved for later use or discarded. Rinse insides and outer areas well under cool running water. Use cloth towel to drain and pat dry.

Approximate Roasting Times when using an oven bag:

Roast 2 to 2-1/2 hours for turkey 12 - 16 pounds
Roast 2-1/2 to 3 hours for turkey 16 - 20 pounds
Roast 3 to 3-1/2 hours for turkey 20 - 24 pounds

However, since oven temperatures do vary, the final judge of timing must be either when the "pop-up" timer is activated; or when the meat thermometer reads 180°F. If turkey is stuffed, add an additional 1/2 hour.

3 With hands, rub vegetable oil onto all outer surfaces of turkey. Sprinkle liberally with poultry seasoning, salt and pepper. If you are cooking stuffing inside of turkey, very lightly "stuff" large front cavity at this time. Place turkey in bag. (Some turkeys come with "pop-up" timers to tell you when turkey is done; make sure this is on top when turkey is placed in bag.) If "pop-up" timer not included, insert meat thermometer into thickest part of leg, not touching bone.

4 Close the oven bag securely with nylon tie provided. Cut 6 1/2-inch slits around the top and sides of bag to allow steam to escape. Make sure to cut a slit at the location of timer or thermometer to allow you to see it.

5 Place bag with turkey inside roasting pan; place pan in center of oven, making sure that no part of bag touches walls of oven or heating element.

6 See above chart for roasting times. When roasting is complete, let turkey rest for at least 15 minutes to absorb juices before carving.

7 This Guide is purposely leaving out carving instructions. You will just have to experiment with a sharp knife. There is no "wrong" way to do it!!

mushroom and onion stuffing

2 packages stuffing mix with seasonings (6 ounces each)
1/2 cup butter (1stick)
1 onion, chopped
1 can mushroom pieces (7 ounces), drained
1 can chicken broth (14 ounces)
1 can water (14 ounces)

Serves 10 - 12

1 Melt butter in 3-quart saucepan; add chopped onion and drained mushrooms. Cook over low heat for about 10 minutes. Onions should be limp.

2 Add chicken broth, water and seasonings from stuffing mixes; heat until almost boiling. Remove from heat; stir in stuffing. Cover and let rest for 5 minutes.

3 Transfer to serving dish; serve hot.

4 Note: If not serving immediately, transfer to greased casserole dish; cover and refrigerate. After removing the turkey for carving, re-heat stuffing in hot oven for about 30 minutes.

There is absolutely no reason to toast and cut up your own bread to have scrumptious stuffing. Buy it already packaged, add a few extras, and it will truly taste like homemade. In fact, after you add your own ingredients, it is homemade!

Note: You might want to use part of this double recipe to stuff your turkey, and put the remainder in a pretty casserole dish. Stuff your turkey immediately before roasting and refrigerate remainder to reheat before dinner.

baked ham with pineapple mustard glaze

1 ham, fully cooked, boneless

For glaze and garnish:
1 can pineapple slices
1/2 cup brown sugar
1 tablespoon mustard
Maraschino cherries
Plain wooden toothpicks

Note: Allow for 2 servings per pound of ham. There will be some shrinkage when cooked.

If you have never made a baked ham you will be amazed at how effortless this is. I wish I could be at your table when you receive all of your compliments.

1 Preheat oven to 325°. Remove all packaging materials from ham. Separate pineapple slices from juice, reserving juice for glaze and basting.

2 Place ham in roasting pan. With tip of sharp knife, score the top in a diamond pattern, 1 inch wide by 1/4 inch deep.

3 To make glaze, combine 1 tablespoon of the reserved pineapple juice with brown sugar and mustard. Spread this over top of ham. Bake, uncovered, at 325° for 1 hour.

4 Remove from oven; baste with pan juices and additional pineapple juice. Arrange pineapple slices on top of ham, with maraschino cherry in center of each slice. Secure cherries with toothpicks. Continue to bake, uncovered, an additional 15 minutes.

5 Remove to your prettiest platter; serve hot.

cranberry-orange sauce

1 can whole berry cranberry sauce (16 ounces)
1 can mandarin oranges (11 ounces)

Optional: 1/4 cup pecan pieces for garnish

Serves 6

1 Drain cranberry sauce and mandarin oranges. Using spoon, gently mix together, being careful to not mash berries.

2 Transfer to serving bowl; chill until ready to serve.

3 If desired, sprinkle top with pecan pieces.

The holiday dinner does not seem to be complete without cranberry sauce.

Holidays are the time to use your most beautiful wedding presents. This is the perfect chance to use that lovely small bowl that you didn't know quite what to do with!

sweet potatoes
and marshmallows

2 cans cut sweet potatoes (15 ounces each)
2 eggs
1 teaspoon vanilla
1/2 teaspoon cinnamon
1/2 teaspoon salt

1 bag large marshmallows (10 ounces)

Serves 4 - 6

1 Preheat oven to 350°. Spray or grease 2-quart casserole dish.

2 Drain sweet potatoes well; place in food processor fitted with metal mixing blade. Add eggs, vanilla, cinnamon and salt. Mix until smooth, about 30 seconds. Pour into greased casserole dish.

3 Press marshmallows evenly over sweet potatoes in single layer.

4 Bake at 350°, uncovered, for 30 minutes. Marshmallows should be slightly browned when done.

Another must-have accompaniment for the well dressed holiday table! When you were little, the gooey marshmallows were your favorite. Maybe they still are.

This is easily doubled if you have a large crowd... use a 3-quart casserole dish.

steamed green beans with toasted walnuts

1/2 cup walnuts, pieces or halves

2 bags green beans, frozen (16 ounces each)
1/4 cup butter (1/2 stick)
Salt and pepper

Serves 6 - 8

1 To toast the walnuts: arrange in single layer on ungreased baking pan. Sprinkle liberally with salt and pepper. Bake for 10 minutes at 350°.

2 To prepare green beans: place beans in steamer basket inside large saucepot. Fill pot with enough water to just barely touch the bottom of the basket. Cover pot.

3 Over medium heat, bring water to a boil; continue to cook until beans are hot but still bright green in color, about 10 minutes.

4 Remove steamer basket with beans from pot; discard cooking liquid. Using same pot, toss beans with butter, nuts and salt and pepper to taste. Transfer to serving dish.

Note: if you don't have a steamer basket, cook beans according to package directions. Drain well before mixing with butter and toasted nuts.

Toasting the walnuts is not an absolute must, but it's easy to do and adds a little extra flavor. The "toasting" can be done several days in advance and kept on the counter in a sealed container.

Feel free to substitute pecans or whatever nut you like best.

pumpkin cake

1 box yellow cake mix (18 ounces)
1 can pumpkin (15 ounces)
3 large eggs
1/3 cup vegetable oil

For frosting:
1 can cream cheese frosting (16 ounces)

Optional: 1/4 cup chopped walnuts for garnish

Serves 10 - 12

This pretty cake is the ideal ending to a rich holiday meal.

If you don't have chopped walnuts, any nut would be fine. Or... a maraschino cherry in the center would be festive.

1 Preheat oven to 350°. Spray or grease two 8" or 9" layer cake pans.

2 Combine cake mix, pumpkin, eggs and oil in large mixing bowl (no additional water is needed). With electric mixer on medium speed, beat all ingredients for 2 minutes.

3 Spread evenly in prepared pans; bake at 350° for 35-40 minutes. Let cool for 30 minutes. Remove from pans onto waxed paper; cool an additional 30 minutes before frosting.

4 To frost: Invert one layer of cake onto serving plate (flat side of cake facing up). Cover top only with one-half of the cream cheese frosting; do not frost sides. Invert second layer on top of frosted cake; again cover top only with remaining frosting. If desired, sprinkle chopped nuts on top. After frosting hardens a bit, cover with plastic wrap or foil until ready to serve.

sim'-mer v.

to remain at or just below the boiling point, usually forming tiny bubbles with a low, murmuring sound

Reference: Webster's New World Dictionary of American English, Third College Edition, Copyright © 1988 by Simon & Schuster, Inc. NY

spiced cider

3 quarts apple cider
1 tablespoon whole cloves
2 sticks cinnamon
1 orange, halved and sliced

Serves 10 - 12

1 Put all ingredients in large pot. Simmer on stovetop for at least one hour.

2 Serve with ladle.

When you catch the aroma of this cider, you just know it's a holiday.

If you don't have room on your stovetop (or you need to allow ample space for the turkey when you take it out of the oven), this recipe adapts very well to a slow cooker which can be used on the countertop.

If a slow cooker is used, allow about 2 hours on High or 4 hours on Low.

chocolate
is a necessary
food group

Chocolate

is a necessary food group.

When my friends learned I was writing a guide to entertaining for newlyweds, including an assortment of recipes, they all insisted I include a special section on chocolate. "Is chocolate an aphrodisiac?" I asked, thinking it might have the same reputation as oysters. "No", they replied. "It just tastes great!!" So, here goes... a few of my best chocolate recipes.

cherry chocolate cake

1 box chocolate cake mix (18 ounces)
1 can cherry pie filling (21 ounces)
3 large eggs

For frosting:
1 cup semi-sweet chocolate chips
2 tablespoons butter

Serves 12

Surprise... when you eat this wonderful dessert, you won't be able to see any cherries. It will look and taste just like a rich, moist chocolate cake.

And... I just have to say it one more time... this tastes even better with vanilla ice cream.

1 Preheat oven to 350°.

2 Spray or grease a 12-cup non-stick Bundt® pan (or other fluted tube pan).

3 Combine chocolate cake mix, cherry pie filling and eggs in large mixing bowl (no additional water or oil is needed). With electric mixer on medium speed, beat all ingredients for 2 minutes.

4 Pour into prepared pan and bake at 350° for 45 minutes. Let cool for 30 minutes; invert onto serving plate.

5 For frosting: Combine chocolate chips and butter in large glass measuring cup; microwave for 1 minute. Stir until smooth. Pour evenly over top of cake, allowing melted chocolate to run down sides. Smooth with edge of knife.

chocolate cream

1 package chocolate instant pudding and pie filling (4 ounces)

2 cups light cream, well chilled

Optional garnish: Whipped cream topping and/or maraschino cherries

Makes 4 one-half cup servings

1 Combine pudding mix and light cream in mixing bowl.

2 Beat with electric mixer at lowest speed for about 1 minute. Pudding mix should be completely blended with cream and slightly thickened.

3 Pour into 4 dessert bowls or use your wine stemware. Cover each portion with plastic wrap; chill for at least one hour before serving.

4 If desired, garnish with whipped cream topping and/or maraschino cherries.

The secret to the creaminess of this recipe is using light cream instead of milk as directed on the package. If you want a richer chocolate flavor, use chocolate fudge instant pudding and pie filling.

Note: To measure and mix in one step, use a 1-quart measuring container as a mixing bowl.

When you have very little time and need a dessert that everyone loves, make fudge brownies... from a mix! Yes, from a mix. The secret to success each time is to blend all liquid ingredients, including eggs (usually two), very well before adding the dry mix. Then... follow package instructions. What about a sprinkle of sliced almonds or chopped pecans on top before baking? Cover tightly when cool; no need to refrigerate. Brownies should stay fresh for several days.

For a special treat, serve with the ice cream of your choice and/or additional ice cream toppings purchased from your local grocer.

peanut chocolate bars

1/2 cup butter (1 stick)
1 cup graham cracker crumbs
1 cup coconut, flaked
2 cups semi-sweet chocolate chips (12 ounces)
1 cup peanuts
1 can sweetened condensed milk (14 ounces)
(not evaporated)

Makes 48 large bars or 24 small bars

1 Preheat oven to 350°.

2 While oven is heating, melt butter in 9"x13" baking pan.

3 Place on top of melted butter, in even layers, all remaining ingredients as listed, beginning with the graham cracker crumbs and ending with the sweetened condensed milk. Pour the condensed milk slowly to dribble over entire top. It won't seem as if it's enough but it is. Use the back of a spoon to smooth nuts and chocolate.

4 Bake at 350° for 30 minutes. Let cool.

5 Cut into bars. Store, tightly covered, in the refrigerator or freezer.

This is also great as a munchie while watching a sporting event.

If you want to crush the peanuts slightly, use the bottom of a glass on a sheet of waxed paper.

chocolate peanut butter **fudge**

1 large package semi-sweet chocolate chips (12 ounces)
1 large package cream cheese (8 ounces)
2 tablespoons butter
1/2 cup creamy peanut butter
1 tablespoon vanilla extract
1 box powdered sugar

Makes approximately 64 pieces

Everybody likes fudge. This is a good treat to keep in the freezer for unexpected guests.

This particular recipe is one of the very few fudge recipes which can be made without cooking. If you prefer, use a heavy-duty stand mixer instead of the food processor.

1 Grease a 9"x9" baking pan and set aside.

2 Melt chocolate chips in microwave about 1 minute on High power. Add cream cheese and butter; heat 1 more minute. Transfer to food processor fitted with metal mixing blade.

3 Add peanut butter and vanilla extract to chocolate mixture; blend until smooth. Gradually add powdered sugar; continue to process until all ingredients are completely blended. If processor slows down or if your workbowl is small, remove part of the fudge and process in batches.

4 Spoon into greased baking pan. Cover; chill for about 2 hours. Cut into 1-inch squares.

chocolate popcorn

1 package "microwave" popcorn

1 cup semi-sweet chocolate chips
1/4 cup butter (1/2 stick)

Waxed paper

Make a big pitcher of daiquiries to go with this quick and easy popcorn.

Have a salt shaker nearby.

1 Prepare popcorn in microwave as package directs.

2 Spread finished popcorn in shallow pan lined with waxed paper; remove all unpopped kernels.

3 Using a small saucepan over low stovetop heat, melt butter. Add chocolate chips and continue to heat, stirring until chocolate is completely melted and smooth. Using a spoon, drizzle chocolate over popcorn.

4 Place pan of popcorn in freezer for 10 minutes until chocolate is hardened. Break apart and place in serving bowl.

chocolate-dipped strawberries

1 quart large, ripe fresh strawberries

1 cup semi-sweet chocolate chips
1/4 cup butter (1/2 stick)

Waxed paper

This is a fabulous dessert during strawberry season. Easy and elegant! Can be made in advance and kept chilled.

Serve with a selection of purchased cookies. Shortbread or sugar cookies would be a good choice.

1 Wash berries and set on paper towel to drain and dry. Leave green stems attached. Cover cookie sheet with waxed paper for later use.

2 Using a small saucepan over low stovetop heat, melt butter. Add chocolate chips and continue to heat, stirring until chocolate is completely melted and smooth.

3 One at a time, holding berry by stem, dip fruit into chocolate, twirling to coat middle and bottom. Set on cookie sheet and refrigerate until ready to serve.

When strawberries are out of season, this same technique can be used with other fresh fruit or dried fruit, such as large apricots. Experiment with different selections.

For variety, how about dipping a big cookie? Or... using white chocolate?

party themes

chili (or soup) plus...

Chili (or soup) plus.... this is a variation on potluck (further described later in this chapter) which is a very easy, inexpensive way to entertain a large group of assorted friends and family. You, as hosts, will provide a mega-amount of chili or soup (recipes start next page) which can be prepared in advance and kept warm on the stove for many hours. But... that's the only thing you will have to make. Each guest will be asked to bring an appetizer or dessert of their choice. It is amazing to see the wonderful goodies they will happily surprise you with at the door!

Plan on providing one quart of soup or chili for every four guests. For 8 quarts, you will need at least a 10-quart pot.

Note: At this type of party, hosts usually provide the necessary basics, including paper plates, napkins, cups, eating and serving utensils, and drinks. Appropriate rolls and chips or crackers would also be nice to have on hand.

Choose a day or evening when most people are not working (such as New Years or your favorite sports event) and wanting an occasion to celebrate. If there are a lot of people coming, designate the party to be "open house" and offer a broad range of time, such as 1 to 5, so the crowd will be staggered.

Keep the chili or soup warm over very low stovetop heat, put everything else on the kitchen table, and invite guests to help themselves while you enjoy the party.

chili
for a crowd

3 pounds ground beef
1 large onion , chopped
2 large cans diced tomatoes (28 ounces each)
3 packages chili seasoning (1 ounce each)

Optional:
2 cans kidney or pinto beans, drained (15 ounces each)

Optional garnish: shredded Cheddar cheese

Serves 10 - 12

1 Brown ground beef and chopped onion in large stock pot. Use wooden spoon to mash and separate meat, until crumbly. Drain any excess fat.

2 Add tomatoes, chili seasoning and drained beans, if desired. Mix well to combine. Simmer over medium heat for approximately 10 minutes. Cover; keep warm over low heat.

3 Optional garnish: Provide shredded Cheddar cheese in nearby bowl for guests to help themselves.

pumpkin bisque
with ginger

3 cans pumpkin (15 ounces each)
2 cans chicken broth (14 ounces each)
1/4 cup sugar
2 cups heavy cream
4 cups milk
1/4 cup quick-mixing flour (such as Wondra®)
2 teaspoons ground ginger
1/2 teaspoon white pepper
1 teaspoon salt

Optional garnish: dried basil

Serves 10 - 12

This is a wonderful soup to serve to a large crowd since it is so flavorful and so easy.

If your expected group of guests is very large, double the recipe.

Remember... this is all you will have to make.

1 Purée pumpkin, chicken broth and sugar in food processor. (This may have to be done in batches.)

2 Transfer to large stock pot. Add cream, milk, flour, ginger, white pepper and salt; stir well with wire whisk. Bring to a boil over medium heat. Lower heat and continue to simmer for about 10 minutes, stirring as necessary to prevent mixture from sticking to bottom of pot. Bisque will become slightly thickened.

3 Keep warm over low heat; do not allow to boil. Bisque may continue to thicken as it is heated. If desired, add a little milk to thin.

4 Have a small bowl filled with dried basil nearby for guests to help themselves to garnish.

meatball and tortellini chowder

Prepared meatballs, frozen (24 - 32 ounces)
Pre-cooked cheese tortellini, frozen (16-24 ounces)

1 can crushed tomatoes (28 ounces)
1 jar or can spaghetti sauce (26 ounces)
10 cups water
1 cup red wine
1/4 cup parsley flakes
1 tablespoon garlic powder
1 tablespoon beef bouillon
1/2 teaspoon ground red (cayenne) **pepper**

Garnish: shredded mozzarella cheese

Serves 12 - 16

Another excellent soup to serve to a large group of family and friends. The ingredients are relatively inexpensive considering you are feeding so many people.

It would be nice to have garlic bread available. Guests will be bringing everything else.

1 Thaw meatballs and cut in half; set aside.

2 Using a large stock pot (10-quart or larger), add crushed tomatoes, spaghetti sauce, water, wine, parsley, garlic powder, bouillon and red pepper. Mix with wire whisk, making sure all seasonings are well distributed. Cook over medium high heat until mixture begins to boil.

3 Lower heat. Add meatballs and tortellini; continue to simmer, stirring as necessary, for about 30 minutes. Cover; keep warm over low heat.

4 Have a bowl filled with shredded mozzarella cheese nearby for guests to help themselves.

it's a wrap

It's a wrap....... this seems to be the latest restaurant craze and there's no reason you can't duplicate the same technique at home. It's another easy and fun way to entertain a small or large group of assorted friends and family. You, as hosts, will provide an ample amount and variety of soft flour tortillas (easily purchased at your local grocers, usually in a refrigerated case near the dairy department) and a variety of fillings and condiments. Guests will serve themselves... making their own wraps... from the selection you have provided.

I suggest that you ask each guest to bring a small appetizer, salad or dessert of their choice to round out the meal. Besides freeing you from the total effort and expense of the entire meal, having guests participate invests them in the success of the evening and everyone will have a better time. In short, guests like to bring something.

Have as much prepared in advance as possible so that you can enjoy the party. A selection of possible foods to include is on the following page, but be sure to add whatever you like.

This is an excellent party at which to use and display all the pretty serving bowls and dishes you received. Mix and match however you like.

Note: At this type of party, hosts usually provide the necessary basics, including paper plates, napkins, cups, eating and serving utensils, and drinks.

Choose a few fillings, a few condiments... and wrap.

for the wrap...

You will need several packages (10" size) of soft flour tortillas; your local grocer should offer a variety of flavors including spinach, sundried tomato, and whole wheat.

for the fillings...

Chopped lettuce
Chopped tomatoes
Sliced red onions
Shredded cheese
Caesar salad (already prepared)
Cooked baby shrimp
Grilled chicken strips
Grilled beef strips
Fajita mix

Shrimp, chicken and beef strips, and fajita mix can usually be purchased in the grocer's frozen section, pre-cooked and ready to heat. Or, simply broil boneless chicken or steak, seasoned with garlic salt and pepper, and slice thinly. For fajita mix, add sautéed slices of onion and green peppers.

for the condiments...

Mayonaise
Mustard
Honey mustard
Ranch dressing
Sour cream
Guacamole
Salsa
Hot sauce

For easiest handling and serving: cut each tortilla in half. Have guests place fillings in middle, fold bottom rounded edge up about one inch and roll together starting at one side. Top will be the straight, cut side of tortilla. Each tortilla will make two small servings.

If you prefer warm tortillas, wrap stack of tortillas in foil and heat for 5 minutes in hot oven prior to serving.

on the grill...

All right grooms, even though I know you have been participating throughout this book, it is now truly your time to shine. The sun is waning, the chores are done, and it's time to heat up the grill. Your guests will be arriving soon and they will be hungry.

Preparing dinner with your outdoor grill is a time-honored way to entertain in a casual manner. It can be as simple as hot dogs and hamburgers with corn-on-the-cob, or something slightly more complicated such as a marinated seafood entrée. Either way... or somewhere in the middle... meal preparation and delivery are usually more casual. If you are lucky enough to have patio furniture, eating outside is always fun. Consider good quality paper or disposable plastic plates and cups to eliminate cleanup. Plastic forks and spoons... why not? Don't forget the knives. Scatter a few of your nicest potted plants around the eating area and arrange container candles for when the sun goes down. Have a bucket of ice available to keep drinks cold without having to go in and out of the house.

Back to basics. If using a time-tested charcoal barbeque grill, use good quality charcoal with a few hickory chips for flavor and not too much fire starter since you don't want your delicious dinner to smell like kerosene. (It's also dangerous if flames get too high). If you are using a gas grill, follow manufacturers' instructions carefully, as they are all a little different. Whichever one you choose (and you can get great results either way) begin heating the grill at least 30 minutes in advance to insure sufficient grill temperature - very hot!

brats and burgers

1 package bratwurst (8 - 10 links)

2 pounds ground beef
1 package dried onion soup (1 ounce)

Hot dog buns
Hamburger buns
Mustard, ketchup

Optional: lettuce, sliced tomatoes, pickles, sliced onions, sliced cheese

Serves 8 - 10

Start off entertaining "on the grill" with old favorites. Add corn-on-the-cob and either cole slaw or potato salad from the deli.

1 Mix ground beef with dried onion soup. Form into patties.

2 Optional: Arrange platter with lettuce, sliced tomatoes, pickles, sliced onions and sliced cheese.

3 When coals are ready, begin grilling brats and burgers. If brats are done more quickly than burgers, move them to the side of the grill away from the coals. Allow at least 10 minutes total cooking time, turning once.

to grill corn-on-the-cob...

Remove all husks and silks from corn and rinse well. Wrap each ear of corn in aluminum foil; place on grill. Cook over hot coals for about 20 - 30 minutes, turning as needed to prevent burning. For faster cooking time, close lid on grill. Serve with salt, pepper and fresh butter.

to grill other vegetables...

including (but not limited to) onions, green or red peppers, mushrooms and eggplant

2 basic methods -

1. Thread small chunks or slices of vegetables on metal skewers; brush with vegetable oil or Italian salad dressing. Grill briefly on hot coals until crisp tender; or,

2. Brush cut vegetables with oil or dressing and place, single layer, on special grill pan; place entire pan on hot coals, turning as necessary. Grill until crisp tender. Slice vegetables thinly to encourage faster cook time.

shish kebab...

Place small pieces of boneless chicken, meat, shrimp or scallops on skewers with vegetables of your choice. Add chunks of pineapple for variety.

marinated salmon

4 salmon steaks
1/4 cup olive oil
1/4 cup lemon juice
1/4 teaspoon garlic powder
Salt and black pepper

Optional: lemon wedges for garnish

Serves 4

1 Prepare grill. (If using charcoal, use minimum amount of starter fluid to preserve delicate taste and aroma of salmon.)

2 While coals are heating, combine olive oil, lemon juice and garlic powder in mixing bowl. Add salmon; coat well on all sides. Let marinate for 30 minutes or until coals are very hot. Sprinkle both sides generously with salt and pepper.

3 When coals are ready, place steaks on grill. Allow at least 10 - 12 minutes total cooking time, turning once. If outside is cooking too quickly, move steaks toward the outer edge of grill where there is less heat. Salmon is ready when it is no longer translucent and slightly flaky.

4 Transfer to a platter and serve. If desired, garnish with lemon wedges.

Almost any seafood is delicious grilled on hot coals. I chose salmon as an example because it is easy to find and almost universally well-liked, but feel free to choose whatever fish you like. The preparation is the same.

If you can, serve with Greek Salad with Feta Cheese and Lemon.

potluck (pat' luk') dinner n.

a dinner to which everyone brings a dish or entrée, salad or dessert to share

Reference: Webster's New World Dictionary of American English, Third College Edition, Copyright © 1988 by Simon & Schuster, Inc. NY

potluck dinner

For the newlywed host and hostess, this is a lucky party indeed. The more people you invite the more and different food you will have, with reduced expense and effort for all.

It is just what Webster's definition says: Each couple brings a favorite dish to share, with the host and hostess giving direction as to what part of the meal it should be. One couple brings salad, another brings dessert... You get the point! Host couple sets table, usually makes the main entrée and provides drinks. You have been to this type of dinner many times... and it has been suggested throughout this book. I just feel this concept is so very important it deserves its own section to fully bring it to your attention.

When your guests ask "what can I bring?"... simply tell them! This is not the time to be shy.

But... it is your party... so you are in charge of organizing who brings what!!

The variations are endless. Everything can be store-bought (such as deli salads or cake from a bakery) or elaborately hand-prepared (such as Grandma's favorite corn soufflé). Same rules apply to the host couple. Make or buy... whatever your schedule and mood allows for. The most important thing is to remember that it is a party so have a good time.

progressive dinner

For this type of a party....... you will need the full cooperation of a group of your friends, for the dinner will actually have several sets of hosts and hostesses. But every party needs an organizer and since you are by now probably getting the reputation of host and hostess extraordinaire, you could volunteer to be Chair Couple.

A progressive dinner is... having each part of the meal at a different home. One couple starts off with drinks and appetizers, the second couple has soup or salad, the next couple has the main entrée, and the last couple has dessert. If there are only three couples, then combine a salad with the main dish. A group of either three or four couples is the optimum amount.

Suggestions: try to plan this event when the weather is more likely to be nice. You don't want to be running around in the snow with freezing temperatures. If the couples all live nearby, it is fun to walk in nice weather. And, if possible have your part of the evening fully prepared in advance so that you can enjoy the party.

At this type of party, each host and hostess is responsible for providing whatever necessary basics are required for their portion of the meal. This would include appropriate plates, eating and serving utensils, drinks, and of course, napkins.

salad bar

Salad Bar...... another variation on the Potluck party, but with a specific theme. Your dining room table will look like an all-you-can-eat salad bar. As hosts, you will provide an ample amount of cut lettuce and a selection of popular salad dressings, served in your most decorative bowls. It would be nice to have one large bowl of crisp iceberg lettuce and another bowl of mixed greens. Your guests will be responsible for bringing anything and everything else to complete the salad "bar". The amounts they should bring of each item will vary according to how many guests are participating.

I suggest that you, as hosts, have a master list of items you would like for your salad bar and allow guests to choose what they would like to bring, accordingly. It might be necessary to have guests bring two or three items each.

Possible items to be included are as follows:
Tomatoes, shredded or cubed cheeses, sliced meats, marinated vegetables, garbanzo beans, bacon crumbles, sliced hardboiled eggs, pineapple chunks, sliced beets, sliced carrots, sliced cucumbers, sliced pepper strips, mushrooms, olives and croutons

This is a particularly easy party. It is suggested that guests bring their salad items already in serving containers, ready to put on the table.

If you serve on disposable plates, be sure to buy the sturdy variety.

Note: In addition to having sturdy plates, hosts should provide napkins, cups, eating utensils, drinks, rolls and dessert.

the white elephant

This party is a must for all newly married couples. The host couple and all invited guests each bring one, two, three or more unwanted wedding presents that you (they) have no use for and/or don't have a clue what they are. All married couples have such gifts! One couple's discard might be another couple's treasure. It works best if all couples bring the same amount of presents to exchange. The fun is in the switching.

You as host couple need to provide the rules as to how the gifts are exchanged. You might give each couple play money that you can get at a toy store... or make your own. Host and hostess can be the auctioneers. Or... put all contributed presents in the middle of the room and give each couple a number and let them take turns choosing what they want. A twist on this method is for each successive guest to have the option of taking what has already been chosen by the guest before. So, it would happen that a higher number (choosing last) is better than a lower number (choosing first). It's always fun to have everyone guess what are the possible uses of the various items.

Because this party is the most fun with four or more couples, be sure to provide an easy-to-prepare and inexpensive dinner. Hot dogs and corn-on-the-cob would be a good choice. Add cole slaw or baked beans if you like. Or... bring in a few pizzas and make a big green salad. Make brownies from a mix for dessert. Whatever you do, I beg you to keep it simple.

Be sure not to plan this event on the evening of a favorite sports event on television.

I think the description disguises the potential hilarity of this party. And... everyone will go home with one or more "new" presents.

I can't believe it... this Guide is done, ready for print. You darling brides and grooms have been in my every thought this past year as I have been writing this book for you. I feel as if I know you all... I have tried to picture myself in your kitchens, living rooms and dining rooms. I have attempted to think your thoughts, hear your exclamations... and yes, even hear your doubts and frustrations. I have wanted this Newlyweds Guide to Entertaining to be just right for you.

I would love to hear from you. E-mail me and let me know what you like, what you don't. Or... if you have a question... please let me know and I will do my best to personally answer you.

I thank you again for allowing me to be a part of your entertaining as you begin your new lives as newlyweds. Remember... relax, enjoy, have fun! SGK

E-mail: bridalguide@hotmail.com

Index to Recipes, by Chapter

The Main Event, continued

Accompaniments

Desserts

Three Ingredients or Less

Appetizers

Entrées

What A Crock

Holidays

Chocolate is a Necessary Food Group

Party Themes

Note: Every effort was made throughout this book to respect and denote appropriate trademarks for registered products whose use has been suggested.